Priests Are People, Too!

Priests Are People, Too!

Thomas M. Kane

Foreword by Ronald Rolheiser, O.M.I.

ThomasMore®
– An RCL Company –
Allen, Texas

Send all inquiries to:
Thomas More® Publishing
An RCL Company
200 East Bethany Drive
Allen, Texas 75002-3804

Telephone: 800-264-0368 / 972-390-6300
Fax: 800-688-8356 / 972-390-6560

Visit us at: **www.thomasmore.com**
Customer Service E-mail: **cservice@rcl-enterprises.com**

Printed in the United States of America

Library of Congress Control Number: 2001 135472

7474   ISBN 0-88347-474-3

1 2 3 4 5   05 04 03 02 01

Dedication

This book is dedicated to my mother and father who raised my siblings and myself not just to be good kids, but quality adults. Thank you! I love you both.

Acknowledgments

I WOULD LIKE to thank God for surrounding me with the people who helped make this book possible. I am indebted to my wife Lee Ann, who has the patience of a saint. I know that throughout this project she had to tap into that patience many times. And to my daughter Lindsay, who kept this book a secret for almost three years. I love you both so much.

A heartfelt thank-you to my dear friends, Joe Sabo and Doug and Katie Fisher, who freely gave of their time to assist me with this book. Joe began this journey with me and was a continuous source of encouragement and counsel. From proofreading to computer support, Joe was always there. Doug and Katie are two extraordinarily gifted people who spent countless hours editing every word of this manuscript. I look up to them as Catholics and I am honored to call all three of them my friends.

A special thanks to Father Ronald Rolheiser, O.M.I., for writing the foreword, and to Brother Patrick Hart, O.C.S.O., and Dr. Maureen O'Brien, Ph.D., for their assistance with this book and their willingness to be involved.

Finally, I must express my gratitude to John Sprague and Debra Hampton of Thomas More Publishing. Their wisdom and insight have made this experience truly enjoyable.

Contents

Foreword

WHAT MAKES for a priest? What constitutes priesthood? What might draw someone into the ranks of ordained ministry?

One of America's foremost theological and spiritual writers, Michael Buckley, once preached a homily at the first Mass of a young man who had just been ordained. Buckley's challenge to the young man was not, Are you strong enough to be a priest? Rather, his question was, Are you weak enough to be one? Are you ordinary enough as a person to give incarnation, real human skin and expression, to the hospitality, service, and fidelity of God?

Here's how Buckley worded this challenge: "There is a question at the very essence of the priesthood; uniquely proper to it: Is this man weak enough to be a priest? Is this man deficient enough so that he cannot ward off significant suffering from his life, so that he lives with a certain amount of failure, so that he feels what it is to be an average man? Is there any history of confusion, of self-doubt, of interior anguish? Has he had to deal with fear, come to terms with frustrations, or accept deflated expectations? These are critical questions, and they probe for weakness. Why? Because, according to Hebrews, it is in this deficiency, in this interior lack, in this weakness, that the efficacy of the ministry and priesthood of Christ lies.

"There is a classic comparison running through contemporary philosophy between Socrates and Christ, a judgment between them in human excellence. Socrates went to his death with calmness and poise. He accepted the judgment of the court, discoursed on the alternatives suggested by death and on the dialectical indications of immortality, found no cause for fear, drank the poison, and died. Jesus—how much the contrary. Jesus was almost hysterical with terror and fear: "with loud cries and tears to him who was able to save him from death." He looked repeatedly to his friends for comfort and prayed for an escape from death, and he found neither. Finally he established control over himself and moved into his death in silence and lonely isolation, even into the terrible interior suffering of the hidden divinity, the absence of God.

"I once thought that this was because Socrates and Jesus suffered different deaths, the one so much more terrible than the other, the pain and agony of the cross so overshadowing the release of the hemlock. But now I think that this explanation, though correct as far as it runs, is superficial and secondary. Now I believe that Jesus was a more profoundly weak man than Socrates, more liable to physical pain and weariness, more sensitive to human rejection and contempt, more affected by love and hate.

"Socrates never wept over Athens. Socrates never expressed sorrow and pain over the betrayal of friends. He was possessed and integral, never overextended, convinced that the just person could never suffer genuine hurt. And for this reason, Socrates— one of the greatest and most heroic people who has ever existed, a paradigm of what humanity can achieve within the individual— was a philosopher. And for the same reason, Jesus of Nazareth was a priest—ambiguous, suffering, mysterious, and salvific."

Yes, Jesus was a priest, not a philosopher, not superman. The Gospels make this clear. They speak of Jesus' extraordinary power, but they talk too of his humanity, of his being ordinary, of his both enjoying and suffering the normal, everyday things of this life. Priests are meant to be like Jesus in this. Ordinary life, his own and that of the world, is what a priest is meant to offer to God each day in sacrifice. The priesthood is not about extraordinary individuals, having the blood of gods, empowered beyond the rest of us, rendered fit to offer proper prayer and sacrifice to God because they are immune from the joys, sorrows, and weaknesses of the ordinary person. That wouldn't describe Jesus or his priesthood.

Indeed, even given the fact that the Gospels often highlight the humanity of Jesus, a priest is not even up to the task of properly incarnating what Jesus, as a priest, did. Nobody does Jesus real well! Nobody, clerical or lay, is up to that task, but each priest can shape God's boundless energy and blessings in a unique way. This is what lies at the essence of the priesthood and is what beckons ordinary persons toward this vocation.

Pierre Teilhard de Chardin was a famous scientist and writer, but he was, too, a Jesuit priest, and a very good one. For him, it was important each day to hold the world, in all its beauty and all its pain, up to God—for God's glory, for God's blessing, and for God's healing. In the bread, he saw the world's achievements; in the wine, he saw the world's pain: "In a sense the true substance to be consecrated each day is the world's development during that day—the bread symbolizing appropriately what creation succeeds in producing, the wine (blood) what creation causes to be lost in exhaustion and suffering in the course of that effort." This is true priestly prayer for the world.

Today we are in desperate need of priests to serve in the church, just as we are also in desperate need of married persons and single persons who, by their hospitality, service, and fidelity, continue to give fresh flesh and expression to the priesthood of Jesus Christ. A wondrous, challenging invitation lies too much unanswered: The eternal priesthood of Christ wants your energy, your heart, and your face to give it shape today.

This little book, *Priests Are People, Too!,* by Thomas M. Kane, is a labor of love. He interviewed more than two thousand priests to compile the stories that fill its pages. That was the labor. His expression, his tone, and what he ultimately selected to share are the love. The book is a compilation of the tears, the laughs, the intensity, the boredom, and the extraordinary and ordinary in-breaking of grace that makes up the real world of priests. I am a priest. I can vouch for these stories.

And this is a needed book—indeed, a courageous one. In a time of anti-clericalism, a time when more men have left the priesthood than are now entering it, a time when too many people make an unconscious association of images between "priest" and "pedophile," when morale among priests often isn't very high and there is a current of cynicism about the priesthood, even among priests themselves, stories like those in this book can sound overly romantic, a throwback to another, more innocent time, "Going My Way—Revisited."

But that isn't the case here, not just because the book shares honestly about struggles and complexities inside the priesthood, but because its stories, in the end, are stories of real faith, gritty faith, faith that is anything but naïve. They are presented by a man who holds the banner of his own faith at good height, at an idealistic height, where faith ultimately belongs.

In a talk to seminarians in Germany some twenty years ago, Pope John Paul II challenged them precisely toward idealism in the priesthood: "There are those who propound an image of the priesthood that would enshrine human weakness as a fundamental principle and declare that it is a human right. Well, we will always be weak, but Christ taught us that, first of all, everyone has a right to his or her own greatness."

These stories, lovingly rendered, invite us to what is best inside the priesthood.

Ronald Rolheiser, O.M.I.
Toronto, Canada
November 12, 2001

Did I Wake You, Father?

The DOORBELL RINGS. I may be discussing some important matter on the telephone, or be in the midst of a counseling session, but if I don't answer that doorbell immediately, I may be greeted with: "Oh, Father, did I wake you from your nap?"

In addition to the nap question, I've sometimes been asked (even by my own sister), "Just what do you *do* all day?"

Many people have no idea what a priest does with his time. So let me give you an idea.

One recent morning I crawled out of bed at 6:00 A.M. for a quick shower and shave. By 6:30 I was praying the Divine Office. Breakfast followed while I watched the morning news, then it was time to prepare for the children's liturgy.

From 9:00 A.M. to noon I taught at the parochial high school. After lunch I attended a workshop for clergy at the local hospital on ministering to the terminally ill and their families. The workshop was over by 5:30 P.M.

During the dinner hour I visited hospitalized parishioners. From 7:00 P.M. to 9:30 P.M. I attended a meeting of the local clergy.

By the time I arrived back at the rectory it was 10:30 P.M. and I was weary. Then the pastor asked me to take a funeral the next morning. He had gotten on the outs with a bereaved family, he explained, and they did not want him to preside. He felt badly, but priests, doctors, and nurses soon learn that outbursts of anger from family members are common, especially in cases of sudden or accidental deaths.

In any case, I now would have to prepare a homily that would soothe some hurt feelings. To complicate matters, I hardly knew the family. After learning as much as I could about them from the pastor, I went to my room to pray and reflect.

The homily was beginning to take shape around 11:30 P.M., when the phone rang. The caller apologized for phoning so late, but she was concerned about her college-age son. He had gotten mixed up with a cult and had decided to drop out of school to spend his life selling flowers for Jesus. After a long phone conversation, the son had agreed to come home to talk things over with his parents, but the cult members insisted they accompany him.

"Would you come over," the caller asked, "and try to reason with him when they come?"

I assured her that I would, assuming it would be some time over the weekend. Our conversation ended, and I returned to my homily. Around 12:50 A.M. I finished and prepared to hit the sack.

I had just dozed off when the phone rang at 1:00 A.M. It was the woman who had called earlier. "They're here," she said. "Could you come over?"

Crawling out of bed and stumbling into the bathroom, I splashed some cold water on my face, combed my hair, dressed, and drove to the caller's residence.

When I walked into the living room I found it crowded with nine cult members, the son in their midst, and the boy's parents, several of his brothers, an uncle, the sheriff, and his deputy.

What followed was a unique experience for me. We argued, discussed religion, family ties, education, and responsibility, but there was no real communication.

We talked until dawn, getting nowhere. Finally, around 5:30 A.M., the sheriff stood up. "The boy is going to remain here for two weeks," he said. "He owes his parents at least that. Then, if he wishes to rejoin your group, he may. As for the rest of you, I will now escort you out of town."

There were loud protests and a few threats. The boy wanted to go with the group, but his two brothers hustled him off to another room. The sheriff, deputy, and the rest of us eventually succeeded in herding the cult members into the van.

As I left the house, the woman whispered, "Thank you for coming over."

It was 5:50 A.M. when I arrived back at the rectory. I still could grab two hours of sleep. I didn't even bother to undress; I just flopped into bed and closed my eyes.

Minutes later the phone rang. There had been a fatal car accident. A funeral director wanted to know if I would notify family members.

Of all the things a priest is called upon to do, this is the most difficult. I know as I approach a family's home that their lives will never be the same. But I had no choice; I spent the next two hours notifying the parents and siblings of the death of their loved one.

I returned to the rectory at 8:40 A.M. for breakfast, but I was too exhausted to eat. I took a cold shower to wake up, then reviewed my homily and went over to the church. The Mass, the trip to the cemetery, and the luncheon that followed are still a muddled blur.

Around 3:00 P.M., some thirty-three hours since I had last slept, I stumbled upstairs and slumped into my easy chair. I couldn't sleep. A few minutes later the doorbell rang.

I plodded downstairs, and when I finally opened the door I was greeted by a cheerful voice: "Did I wake you from your nap?"

Obviously, not all days are like this. Sometimes life is downright boring. But usually there are more things to do than one can accomplish in a day. I may sit at my desk with the intention of spending an hour or two on correspondence, but before I get the first letter written the phone is ringing, someone is at the front door, and somebody else may be at the back door. The person at the door may be a six-year-old with a bouquet of dandelions or someone with a major problem: a victim of spouse abuse, a bereaved person, a parent whose teenage son or daughter has run away, or someone coming to set a date for marriage.

There are sick people and shut-ins to visit. There are administrative responsibilities. There are convert instructions, marriage preparation classes, adult education programs, homilies, meetings, and hundreds of other chores.

I learned a long time ago that, on those rare mornings when I check my calendar and see I have no appointments, I'd better watch out. Within minutes all "heck" may break loose.

But this is what I enjoy so much about the priesthood. Every day is an adventure; no two days are ever the same. A phone call or doorbell ring can literally change the direction of a person's life.

When I was in high school I was shy and reserved. Never in my wildest dreams did I expect to be doing what I now am called upon to do. Other priests would agree. One colleague I know hadn't completed his first week in his first assignment when he was asked to talk to a man who had gone berserk and was threatening to kill himself. For several anxious hours my friend talked to the man before the guy finally calmed down and surrendered his weapon. Another priest climbed a water tower to talk somebody out of jumping. Most priests have been in similar, though not as dramatic, situations.

Yet the greatest joy and privilege of priestly ministry is being able to share in the lives of our parishioners. People share their innermost problems, their worries and concerns, their suffering and crosses. To be so trusted, to share so intimately in people's lives, is indeed a privilege.

So what if some think we nap all day? It's a small price to pay for the privilege of being a priest.

Father Joseph A. Miksch
Archdiocese of Omaha

1

"Remember, God is watching!"

You, a Priest?

Why WOULD SOMEONE BECOME a priest? When you hear the word "seminary," do you envision a campus full of pious men engaged in reverent prayer?

WITH OVER forty-six thousand priests in the United States alone, I would imagine there would be an equal number of reasons for someone to enter the priesthood. Through the course of this book, I have spoken with priests who realized their calling by eight years of age and others who were called much later in life—these were tagged "second-career men."

Although their reasons vary, they answered the call nonetheless. For some, the decision was made at such an early age that doubt was never a consideration. Others, however, have struggled. Some continue to struggle. The apprehension some of these men experience is common and, perhaps, even gives them a greater commitment to serve God and his people.

They all entered seminary, not simply to study for a degree, but to prepare for a way of life, for a transformation, one might say. And, believe me, seminaries were far different years ago than they are now. But now that it's been many years since these men graduated, they tend to be much more philosophical as they reflect back on their student days. The memories of times shared with friends, of camaraderie and fellowship, of struggles and uncertainty, last a lifetime.

Many of the priests with whom I spoke shared stories not so much of their calling, but of the humorous reactions of friends and family. And they easily reminisced about the escapades and antics that went on in seminary. In no way did they want to debase the institution, but they chose rather to recall specific episodes they still remember fondly. Sound familiar?

THIS MONTH brought an invitation to speak at a regional meeting of Serra Club International, a Roman Catholic lay group that seeks to foster vocations to the priesthood and religious life. My hometown diocese of Erie, Pennsylvania, was playing host to several clubs from Buffalo, Cleveland, and Pittsburgh. They asked me to respond to a simple, straightforward question—"Why did you decide to be a priest?"

One would think that I, like any priest, would have no difficulty in providing a ready answer. Yet, as often as I have put pen to paper this week, there always remains something inexpressible, even mysterious, about the logic and flow of events that lead to ordination. There is a popular belief that a decision for the priesthood, ministry, or religious life must be accompanied by some sort of sign from God. The trouble with signs is that one usually assumes they must be supernatural, something quite out of the ordinary. I had no such sign. For me, the call came from the common, everyday experiences of life. In fact, I have come to understand that we are never nearer God's plan for us as when we are attentive to the familiar details of our daily routines.

For me, it was going to college while working for my dad at a local Coca-Cola bottling company. Crashing a forklift into a stack of empties was just one of a series of signs that I should take my book-learning more seriously. Long interested in the theater, I acted in the evenings with community and university playhouses. I also marched with the Pershing Rifles in ROTC, dated my high-school sweetheart, Susan Rickloff, and started to talk seriously with friends about the future. In the midst of all this, Christ started interfering with everything.

Looking back, I appreciate what Therese of Lisieux meant in *The Story of a Soul* when she admitted that Christ was most abundantly present to her not "during my hours of prayer . . . but rather in the midst of my daily occupations." It almost seemed like a conspiracy. There was Father Frank Haas, a counselor at Gannon University: "Tom, have you ever thought of being a priest?" No one had ever asked me that before. Then Monsignor Louis Lorei, the Dean of Humanities: "Sure, you might want to think about going into education or the theater, but just imagine what you could accomplish as a priest who teaches theater." And then came those serious late-night conversations with friends who showed enthusiasm for the idea: "You, a priest? Yeah, I can see you doing that."

Going to Sunday liturgy became different. Rather than silently criticizing the celebrant for the way he was saying Mass, I began to imagine what I would do or say to make it more meaningful. Presumptuous thinking for a college freshman, but intriguing nonetheless. In time, such imagining turned into reality. But that initial calling still remains a mystery. I can point to the people whose example and gentle prodding helped me imagine the improbable. But the mystery remains, twenty-eight years a priest—and still I marvel how the little things in life become the hinges on which life turns. A chance remark, a tap on the shoulder, a compliment, a gentle nudge—and life is never the same again.

> † *Monsignor Thomas McSweeney*
> *Archdiocese of New York*

I WENT to the seminary when I was fourteen years old. I'm a "lifer." That's the name they called us if we went to the seminary right out of grade school. Back in the fifties, I had an eighth grade teacher, a sister, who encouraged us to go to the seminary just to look at it.

She used to say, "You can't practice being married, but you can go to the seminary to see if it fits."

> † *Father C. Louis Martin*
> *Archdiocese of Baltimore*

I GIVE THANKS for my parents who gave me faith and shared their approach to church. Their practice of going to church and home prayer gave me a foundation of faith. Often they expressed their appreciation for the work of the priest.

Throughout life I have been inspired by priests. Each in his way was a model of the priesthood for me. The pastors at our country church, each with a different charisma, were a magnet for me.

21

The priest who taught religion and coached basketball at the Catholic high school made a deep impression on me. Seminary priest professors led me on the path to the priesthood.

Many times I have been asked, "Why did you become a priest?" Two years ago I found the answer—John 15:19: "I have chosen you." Now I ponder other questions. Why did God choose me to be a priest? Why did he not choose boys who were better with schoolwork and holier than me?

Let me tell you how God worked with me. During preschool years, when the family returned home from Sunday Mass, I would open the oven door, put a cup there, and sing the Mass.

While serving as an altar boy, I wanted to say Mass like the priest. At Catholic high school I was intrigued with the stories the sisters told about missionary priests.

God kept working on me to become a priest. Now let me tell you how I worked with God:

I said to God, "Not yet." I had observed that the smart students, those who studied Latin in high school, were always complaining about the difficulty of Latin study.

So I said to God, "Try again next year. I will till the soil and milk cows for a year." In a year I grew up. I turned eighteen. Then I said yes to entering the seminary.

But God did not hand me the priesthood. I had to earn it through the hardship of studying Latin, Greek, Hebrew, German, and French. That was only the preparation for philosophy and theology with Latin textbooks, lectures, and tests.

Over the years I kept wondering, "Why did God choose me to be a priest?" My final analysis was that he wanted my personality and my talents for some of his work.

Then I asked myself the question, "Who am I?" This is the answer I came up with. God created me to be an adventuresome one who always wanted to see the other side of the mountain and do new things.

God moved me from the farm to the seminary. That was a change of occupation and a change from country to city living. He directed me into the rural missionary diocese of Baker, Oregon, in the Wild West. Finally, God put me in Alaska. God had a way of keeping me going. He exploited my desire for adventure and for seeing the other side of the mountain.

After college and philosophy studies in Milwaukee, I experienced theology studies in Canada with seminarians from around the world. In Oregon, I had a lesson in geography. Assistantships were served in the four corners of the diocese. Each move was a big adventure.

As pastor I served in a high-desert cattle town, at a reservation school and church, at a logging town in the mountains, and at a parish in the fruit orchards along the Columbia River.

Here in Alaska, I had more adventures of travel and work. While traveling as a supply priest, I explored from Cordova to Dutch Harbor and from Seldovia to Glennallen.

It seems quite clear that God had not created me to be a cloistered monk. Besides the curiosity of travel, I had the curiosity of people. And so I say, "Thanks for the association I have had with all you wonderful people."

In conclusion, I reflect on the glory and grace of the priesthood. I thank God for using me in his priesthood. I ask his guidance as I continue to bear witness to the mysteries of faith.

† Father A. J. Fisher
Archdiocese of Anchorage

I LAUNCHED into the working world after I graduated from college in 1972. I went into this world and started to find conflict. I was also involved in a community, under the direction of a priest, of about twenty-five people who decided to live together in a deeper commitment. We formed a community around a promise.

I was very involved with this community of people. During the day, I worked full-time for an insurance company. Monday night, after work, was the pastoral team meeting. Tuesday night was our "Life in the Spirit" seminars, with a prayer meeting afterward. That ended at 10:30 P.M. Of course, we didn't go home at 10:30 P.M. We went out to dinner and socialized, shared and enjoyed fellowship until 2:00 in the morning. I got home at 3:00, went to sleep, then got up and went back to work at 8:30 A.M.

Wednesday we took the Life in the Spirit seminars on the road. Thursday night was our meeting for all those who took the promise. Friday night we hung out together. Saturday night we had a coffee house for the younger people in our group. Sunday night we prepared for the Life in the Spirit seminars we gave during the week.

Seven days a week we hung out together!

By the time January came around, guess what the insurance company was saying about my work? We parted ways.

My manager told me, "I think you're called to something else."

† Father Larry J. Hess
Diocese of Allentown

MY MOTHER'S REACTION when I told her on my sixteenth birthday that I had planned to become a priest:

"Well, you've made one woman very happy!"

"You, mother?" I asked.

"No, the one you don't marry!"

† Father James R. Wilson
Diocese of Boise

✝

TALK ABOUT a prediction. I was born in 1954. In those days, the mother stayed in the hospital well over a week. A couple hours after I was born, my father went to visit my mother in her room. My mom was lying in bed, still somewhat groggy from the anesthesia they had given her. She knew my father was present and asked him with her eyes closed, "What did we have?" My father responded, "We had a baby boy."

"Oh, that's good," my mother said. She then proceeded to ask my father the normal questions about the baby's health. "Does he have ten fingers and ten toes?" she asked. "Of course, Rose, everything is fine." She paused, then squeezed my father's hand and said, "Mario, we're not going to send him away to be a priest, are we?"

Later on that day, the doctor came into the room to check on my mother. After he was done checking her out, he said, "Don't worry, Mrs. Julian, we're not going to send your son away to be a priest."

My father has been telling that story since I was born. And to this day, my mother has no recollection of ever asking those questions. I guess it could have been the ether.

✝ *Father Mario F. Julian, O.F.M.*
Archdiocese of Hartford

✝

ONE TIME during my freshman year of college at Saint Meinrad Seminary I did not do as I was told. The dean of students informed us that we were never to enter the seminary kitchen or to take any food from it. Of course, this immediately became a challenge to the ingenuity of seminarians with time on their hands. One Saturday night, a search party went through the kitchen and found all the necessary ingredients for a hot dog roast. We carried the food out to a lake that was excavated back in the thirties as a water supply for the town, the seminary, and the monastery. No more had we gotten a fire going than we saw headlights coming up the road.

"It's the monks! We're dead!" someone yelled.

We stomped out the fire, gathered all the incriminating evidence, and jumped into the bushes to await further developments.

But it wasn't the monks. A teenaged boy and girl emerged from the car, and began to neck passionately. Their ardor was dashed, however, when one of my classmates shouted from the bushes, "REMEMBER, GOD IS WATCHING!" She screamed, they both ran for the car, and drove away as fast as one could when fleeing divine punishment.

I wonder what effect this religious experience had on their future lives!

> † *Father Thomas Extejt*
> *Diocese of Toledo*

IT WAS the fall of 1962, at Saint Paul's Seminary in Ottawa, Ontario. Frank was tall, heavyset, and rough-looking. He always gave the impression of being in a bad humor, but he wasn't really. We could joke with him and even play tricks on him. He'd fly off the handle for a few seconds, then would laugh about it. That's what made it so much fun to place Frank in odd situations.

That year, we wanted to celebrate his birthday in a memorable way. When the fateful day arrived, "friends" asked him to go into town for the afternoon. While he was away, a group of seminarians got together to inflate hundreds of balloons which were placed in his room. It was quite a feat for them to fill up the room with balloons and still be able to shut the door behind them.

When Frank returned to the seminary, everyone was waiting at their assigned post to see how Frank would react when he opened the door to his room. He did not disappoint anyone.

No sooner had he opened the door to his room than a loud, unsettling moan was heard throughout the long hallway. The others looked out of their rooms to see what was going on. Frank had run into the lavatory, grabbed a mop, and was back in his room trying to mop out the balloons. With every swing he took, the balloons would move up and down and side to side, yet they remained in the room.

Frank's room was across the hall from the third-floor fire escape door. He conceived the idea that he could swoop the balloons out of his room, across the hall, through the fire escape door, and down onto the driveway below. He finally convinced a friend to give him a hand.

As the balloons came out the fire escape door, children were returning home from school. When they saw the balloons floating down toward them, they exclaimed, "It's raining balloons!" Many hurried over, trying to grab as many stringless balloons as they could. A few of the children took off their jackets to make some kind of a bag to secure the balloons together. Others gathered the balloons in bundles, throwing dry leaves over them to hide their catch until they could return with bags to retrieve them and take them home.

All in all, we thoroughly enjoyed Frank's birthday party. Deep down, he had appreciated the prank. This became part of our conversations for several weeks afterward.

† Father Roger P. Chabot
Diocese of Portland, ME

MY SEMINARY EXPERIENCE was great. It was really great. I went to the seminary thinking, "This could be it!" I thought maybe this is what the Lord wanted me to do.

I figured I had four years to think about what I was doing. Most engagements are only a year or two nowadays, so I thought four years was plenty of time to determine if I should become a priest.

I went to the seminary thinking I had plenty of time to discern. But every guy in my class had this kind of "confidence" that they knew they were going to become a priest. I thought to myself, "I'm not that sure, but I want to be like these guys!" You know, peer pressure sets in. I wanted to be confident, too!

However, the doubts started coming like crazy. I kept saying, "Stop that, doubts! I want to be confident like everyone else." The doubts got worse and worse and worse. It was to the point where I actually questioned if God really existed. That's how bad it got!

Then I remembered a conversation I had had with a spiritual director years before when my girlfriend broke up with me. I asked him how to handle the depression, the aloneness, and the hurt. I asked the director if I should be grabbing onto Jesus' hand so it wouldn't pull me under, or should I put Jesus out in front of me like a shield? He said, "Let that depression, let that hurt, and let that emptiness cover you over until you can't lift one finger!" I asked him, "What do you mean, I have to be totally dependent upon God?"

I actually taught that before. That God does raise you up— and he did! In time, he will raise you up from some of the most hurtful situations that you think you can never bear. Because when you do get raised up, you know it's the Lord. You couldn't have done it by yourself.

But the doubts kept coming on like crazy! I went to my room and laid down. I wanted the doubts to cover me over like a blanket. They did cover me over, but they didn't kill me like I thought they would! I rose from that bed with a confidence that was the Lord's. It wasn't mine anymore. At a time of doubt, terrible doubt, the Lord raised me with the confidence to become a priest.

† Father Larry J. Hess
Diocese of Allentown

DAD'S FACE showed no dismay when I told him I would be away for a day to enroll in the seminary. My dad was a staunch Catholic gentleman. He asked, "What can your mother and I do to help you prepare?"

The campus was in a rural setting. The school was a priest factory that trained two hundred seminarians. I vowed to myself to remain a full year, no matter how difficult the Latin studies were!

While in the seminary, I found that our first semester of preaching was the most frightful class. Classroom sermons began the first year of theological training.

As in most seminaries, we had a "class clown." One time, it was his turn to preach in front of the class. We were all wondering what he was going to say.

He got up and stood before the class. He just stood there, and gave a smile and chuckled. As he chuckled, the class began to chuckle. Each time the seminarian started to begin, he just smiled and chuckled. In response, the class chuckled.

It was a hilarious six minutes and the seminarian never preached a sentence.

† Father A. J. Fisher
Archdiocese of Anchorage

THERE WAS ONE THING I was always told in the seminary:
A third of the people are going to love you!
A third of the people are going to hate you!
A third of the people will not even know who you are.

† Father Michael W. Decewicz
Diocese of Pittsburgh

THE SEMINARY taught me nothing about being a pastor! It taught me how to talk about the Trinity, but it never taught me how to fix a boiler, or how to raise the money to have it fixed.

The seminary never taught me how to handle a million dollars. It never taught me how to pay the church bills. Everything was theological and scriptural. The seminary also never taught me how to get money from the bishop.

† Father Mario F. Julian, O.F.M.
Archiocese of Hartford

IN 1966, at the end of the Christmas vacation, I traveled as a young seminarian from my home in Sacramento, California, back to the seminary in Washington, D.C. I was carrying with me a brand-new leather briefcase that I had received as a Christmas gift and of which I was quite proud.

As we deplaned at Dulles Airport, the older gentleman in front of me inadvertently swung his briefcase and chinked a large piece of leather out of my new briefcase. I was immediately incensed at his (perceived) thoughtlessness, and I instantly confronted him.

"Look what you've done!" I exclaimed.

"Oh my," he said, "just call me at the office and I'll replace it." With that, he went toddling off.

I was indignant. Here this total stranger was patronizing me and I still had a seriously damaged briefcase. So, I went charging after him and in a loud voice proclaimed, "Excuse me! I don't know you from Adam. Please give me your name and number."

With that, the gentleman handed me his business card, with some amusement, it seemed. Then he walked away.

I was speechless. However, as I was regaining my wits to make another assault, I had the good sense to look at the business card. It had three words on it: THE CHIEF JUSTICE.

Incidentally, I called the Supreme Court office the next day and explained what had happened. Within a day or two, a Supreme Court courier appeared at the Theological College with a package for me. Inside was a lovely black leather briefcase that was actually much nicer than the original Christmas present I had received.

I carried that briefcase for more than twenty years.

† Father John G. Proctor, Jr.
Diocese of San Diego

I WAS PROBABLY twenty-three or twenty-four years old when I finally realized I could become a priest. Up to that point, I didn't think I was smart enough, holy enough, or good enough.

† Father Edward R. Schleicher
Diocese of Pittsburgh

MY FAMILY'S PARISH LIFE was an extension of our home life. The priests in my parish had a great deal of influence on me.

† Father Paul Hruby
Archdiocese of Los Angeles

WHEN I WENT to the seminary, I thought I was going to be with a bunch of guys who were very holy men. Guys who would never say the word "heck." That's not the way it was at all!

They turned out to be very normal people, very much like myself. There were jokes and sometimes even risqué conversation. That surprised me for about the first month I attended Saint Vincent. I remember saying, "I think I can fit in with this group."

I expected these guys to be really holy people, sort of like monks, but that's not the way it was. The first week we were at football games and playing softball. However, there was a lot of discipline. We weren't allowed to have coffee in our room. We were not allowed to have magazines or newspapers either. If someone came in our room the door had to remain open.

It was very strict. Cars were also forbidden! Now, the seminarians are allowed to have coffeepots, microwaves, TVs, and even cars.

† Father Robert J. Boyle
Diocese of Pittsburgh

"God has an incredible sense of humor. If God called me to be a priest, I know he can call anyone."

Alberto R. Cutie

This MAN REACHES a daily audience of three to five million people. He has had over 780 articles written about him and his radio and television shows by newspapers around the world.

CROWD CONTROL has to be established at many of the airports he arrives in because of his adoring fans. He has been approached by national restaurants, car manufacturers, and many other companies looking for him to endorse their products. Bishops, cardinals, and fellow priests throughout Latin America request his services to help them in their dioceses. Market studies and focus groups have concluded that he has 100 percent recognizability in Latin American countries. But don't dare call him a

star. "I didn't become a star when I went on television; I became a star when Jesus called me to be a priest!" This is the story of Father Alberto R. Cutie (pronounced coo-tee-ay).

Padre Alberto, as he is known throughout the world, is a charismatic thirty-two-year-old priest who has captured the Latin American faithful with his daily radio talk show and weekly television show. Conceived in Spain, born in Puerto Rico, and raised in Miami, he considers himself Cuban American. A priest for only six years, this humble man speaks candidly about the priesthood and the Catholic church. His enthusiastic attitude has energized what is fast becoming the majority of Catholics in the world today, the Hispanic community.

Profile

I WAS BORN on April 29, 1969, in Miami, Florida. My parents are from Cuba but fled to Spain because of the Communist regime. After a short time, my parents arrived in the United States.

I had a very normal childhood growing up in Miami with two sisters. We were what I would call an average Catholic family. My family didn't have intense devotions. We prayed before meals and never missed Sunday Mass, but that was about it. My parents weren't overly churchy people either, but there was always a lot of faith. It was a simple faith. They were friends with our parish priest, but they were not obsessive.

When I was a sophomore in high school, I really started to feel a call to the priesthood. I was only fifteen years old. I went to a public school my whole life, but there were times when I thought of switching to Catholic school. Considering I was so involved with the evangelization of kids, I felt I could reach out to more people by remaining in public school. So I stayed put.

During the same time in my life, I had my own disc jockey business. I played music at parties and weddings, and then I eventually got my own radio program on the public radio in Miami. I loved to dance. My buddies and I always had girl-friends. I guess you could say I was a "ladies' man" when I was a teenager.

I never really thought of priesthood as a child. It happened during my teen years. I began to get involved in parish youth groups and spiritual youth programs. It was the youth encoun-ters and retreats that really enabled me to get to know priests as real people. As I started to get to know the priests and talking with them, I realized more and more that there was definitely an attraction to their life, and to what the priesthood was about. The service, the sacramental life, and the spiritual development were so interesting to me.

I was actively involved in the life of the church as a young person. That got me excited about the mission itself. But the question I kept asking myself was, "What am I going to do with this?" I realized I could take different routes. I could become a committed layman, or a deacon in the future. But the more I ques-tioned myself, and the more I questioned God and what he wanted from me, the more the priesthood kept coming back.

> I didn't think of celibacy as a problem. I thought of celibacy as a challenge.

When I told my friends about my decision to become a priest, the first question they asked me was, "Do you know you're giving up girls?" I told them not to worry because they, too, would be giving up girls one day. I was quick to remind them that the day they get married it becomes "girl." I told them I was making this choice for God. I was choosing to belong to him. That's the only way that celibacy makes any sense to me. When I started thinking of the priesthood, I didn't think of celibacy as a problem. I thought of celibacy as a challenge. It was a sacrifice I wanted to make for God.

My friends, however, did have a lot of fun at my expense. There was a lot of teasing, but that was okay. I have always been the kind of person to laugh at almost everything. So when my friends joked about the priesthood, it was fun. I loved to laugh with them. It was very important for me to have my friends understand that I was still "one of the guys." Fortunately, they always did treat me that way. When they were around me they were also very respectful. If they were cussing one of them would say, "Hey guys, be careful, Father Albert is here." And that was years before I even became a priest.

I still hang out with my old friends and their wives. I've baptized their kids, and I have helped them out over the years. But I've never stopped being just a regular guy. I think that is very important. People need to see priests as human beings.

My parents were very supportive of my decision from the beginning. I had just received my restricted driver's license the day I told my mother. I remember I was driving the car with my mother sitting next to me. She was giving me a hard time about spending too much time partying and too much time with the music and with the guys, and not enough time studying. I was a lazy student when it came to math. It wasn't my favorite subject.

I was driving down a street that at the time would have been considered a rural part of Miami. There were no stop signs, and no red lights. I said, "You know, Mom, I've been wanting to tell you something for some time now. I'm thinking of becoming a priest."

"Hit the brakes!" she yelled.

She doesn't admit it now, but it was a shock for her in the beginning. I have to believe it was such a shock because of how active I was with my friends. I also had a girlfriend at the time, so to come up with that at that point in my life was very unexpected. When I told my mother I was seriously thinking about becoming a priest she said to me, "If it's what God wants, and you are going to be happy, that's what we want for you." And then she gave the typical motherly response, "Talk to your father about it!"

That evening, my father echoed the exact same words as my mother. I received the same supportive attitude from my parents throughout all my years in the seminary.

I attended Saint John Vianney College Seminary in Miami. It was 1987 when I entered, and I was only nineteen years old. Saint John was one of the best places in the world. It was a wonderful seminary and I had a great experience. However, during my sixth year, as I was just completing theology, I received some devastating news. My father was diagnosed with terminal cancer. It was the only time throughout my seminary experience that I considered leaving. I felt I needed to be with my family to help out. When I went home to see my father he said, "No way!

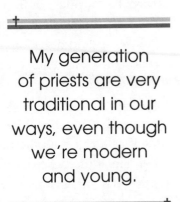

My generation of priests are very traditional in our ways, even though we're modern and young.

Don't leave the seminary. You stick to your vocation and stick to what God wants and we'll be fine. Don't worry about me." My father died in 1993. He was only fifty-four years old.

I like to call the younger generation of priests, and the younger generation going to the seminary today, the John Paul II years, or the restoration years. My generation of priests are very traditional in our ways, even though we're modern and young. Our generation struggled with the lack of orthodoxy in the seminaries. There was almost a lack of seriousness. We wanted more discipline, more prayer, and we wanted more of what the guys in the 1960s were trying to get rid of.

Although in my first four years in the seminary we had the black pants, the white shirt, the discipline, the benediction, and all the basic devotions and traditions, the seminary was still somewhat laid-back. That made the seminary a place that introduced us to Catholic devotional life, because many of our parishes no longer had that stuff. My experience wasn't that rebelliousness of old, "let's burn our cassocks and get rid of the old devotion." My generation wanted those things, and I'd like to think that I represent that generation. Since I was born after the council, I always went to Mass in the vernacular, and I always had a priest in front of me during confession.

I was looking for traditions in the seminary; for depth, seriousness, and devotion. I was looking for a church that some would consider a church of the past. I wear my clerics most of the time. Many of the priests of the past don't wear their clerics regularly, even when they're working. I don't necessarily feel it's a need as much as I feel it's a responsibility. I try to identify myself as a priest all the time. Obviously, when I work out, or when I'm at the beach or I go to the mall, I'm not in my clerics. On my day off, I don't wear a stitch of black at all. I rest. But if I can't go to a place and have a beer in my clerics, then what's the point? Why would I hide? Why would I go dressed in anything else? I believe in the priest as a human being and if people can't get used to it, then they need to be taught.

Prior to my ordination I was an intern. In South Florida, seminarians have an internship for a year before we're ordained. For my internship, I was assigned to Saint Mary, Star of the Sea, in Key West. The church is the southernmost parish in the United States. I was expected to go to the parish full-time. I wasn't in the seminary that semester. All I did was parish work under the pastor's supervision. The following semester I was ordained a deacon. I then went back to finish my course work and began to baptize babies, marry couples, and assist at Mass.

On May 13, 1995, I was ordained a priest of the Archdiocese of Miami. My first assignment was Saint Clement, in Fort Lauderdale. The first day on

> I loved my first assignment. The parishioners were wonderful people.

the job was hilarious. I got to the church and it was a very nice blue-collar parish. It represented what I would call your average American folks. The first thing the pastor said to me was, "Albert, you only have two things to worry about."

"What is that, Father?" I asked.

"Number one, I want you to greet the people outside of every Mass. And number two, just be good to them."

My pastor was a very holy man, and he was correct. The minute I stood outside and greeted people, they started making appointments. They scheduled baptisms and weddings. They were looking for spiritual direction and everything else you can imagine. It was the beginning of a very exciting life. After six weeks with my pastor, he was transferred. I received a new pastor who was much younger than my first. I was also the first associate he ever had. I developed the first Spanish Mass at Saint Clement and it was amazing. I began a youth ministry and established the youth movement. We've had over five hundred kids go through the program, of which I am the spiritual director.

I loved my first assignment. The parishioners were wonderful people and the priests were good men to live with.

We all got along very well. I realize many priests aren't as fortunate. In South Florida, we have a very unique situation with our clergy because there is such an international mix of priests.

The Hispanic community in South Florida encompasses the highest percentage of Catholics in the state. There is also a strong Jewish and Protestant population. We have very few native clergy from the Anglo community because there are very few native Anglo Catholics. Many of the Anglo Catholics relocated to the South from New York, Boston, and Pittsburgh. I was amazed at the number of people who were from Pittsburgh just in Saint Clement alone.

After three years at Saint Clement, I was assigned to Saint Patrick Church in Miami Beach. I was your typical parish priest, busier than life, without time to do anything else. In October of 1998, I received a phone call from a person who asked me if I'd like to "host a program." The program would feature topics about today's youth, family issues, and the church. I figured it was "right up my alley," so why not give it a try.

Once I received approval from my archbishop, I flew to New York to audition for the show. Questions were being fired at me on a variety of subjects that priests deal with every day. This time, however, there was a camera in front of me. After screening hundreds of priests, they chose me to host *"America En Vivo"* (Live in America).

Two and a half years later, in January of 2001, I was assigned to Radio Paz. Radio Paz is the only twenty-four-hour Spanish radio station in the United States. We broadcast in South Florida, but we also have a satellite service, together with Mother Angelica at EWTN, in Alabama. We work in collaboration and we send our signal all through Latin America. We have almost ninety-eight affiliates that are connected to us through different Catholic radio stations throughout Latin America. There are millions of people who are listeners on the radio side. So now I have three jobs: parish priest, television talk show host, and director of the radio station. I still do parish work, but I'm not there every day, all day, like I used to be. Even though I spend more time on the radio, I am still involved in the usual sacrament preparation at Saint Patrick on weekends.

Different cultures express their faith in different ways. The African-American community is so beautiful and so inspirational. Their spirituality is out of this world! Everything happens around the church in the Hispanic world. In our society, the church is the central place. In all of our towns, no matter where you go, Central America, South America, or Mexico, you would see that the church is at the center of the city or the center of the town. It is considered the highlight building of the area. Everyone does their activities around the church. That holds true even today, and that's one of the reasons for the success of the show.

The Hispanic world, as in other cultures, has varying spirituality. Some people want a more traditional church. Actually, many Hispanics don't go to Spanish Mass. They don't want to hear what the Spanish liturgical music has become. Some people think a Hispanic Mass has just guitars and bells. That's not what Spanish liturgical music is like. Most Spanish and Latin American countries are very much for the organ and traditional hymns, the chant. When Hispanics come to America, they want to connect strongly with their roots. Because they're so far away from their homeland, some churches tend to exaggerate the casual Spanish liturgical music. Some Hispanics resent that, so they just prefer to go to an English Mass with an organ.

In the Latin market, the padre is somebody who can always give advice, or someone to turn to with difficulties and struggles. Since most of our countries are 90 percent or more Catholic, there's a real sense of the priest as being one of the leaders of the community. He is listened to and respected the most by our people, even by political and civic leaders. The priesthood in the Hispanic communities still brings honor to the families. There is a sense of, "Wow, one of your sons is considering the priesthood? That's a great thing." However, certain segments of the Hispanic community are becoming more like American society. Some folks have begun to question everything.

The first thing I would tell any young man considering the priesthood is that God has an incredible sense of humor. If God called me to be a priest, I know he can call anyone. It's important to realize that God will work in you if you let him. God respects our freedom a great deal. God will never push you. He will only gently tap you on the shoulder. If you respond, you will be the happiest person in the world. I know that my vocation was not my idea. I believe it started in the heart of God. So for me to follow it was a natural by-product. There is no way I could have come up with the idea of priesthood even if I tried. It's taken me years to discover it, but my vocation is a gift from God.

> Those who think celibacy is the reason for the lack of vocations are mistaken.

It's perfectly natural for anyone who is considering the priesthood to question celibacy. "Welcome to humanity," I tell them. Part of life is making choices. When I chose to be a priest, and when I accepted celibacy as part of my life, I knew it wasn't going to be easy. There are times it hasn't been. But it doesn't mean that celibacy is the greatest sacrifice in the priesthood or the greatest difficulty. There are other things that are equally as challenging. Dealing with certain elements of society and the world is much harder than dealing with celibacy. Celibacy is a natural extension of what the priesthood is all about. The priest offers sacrifice. That's where the word "priest" comes from—one who offers sacrifice. The priest is one who is sacramentally united in an intimate relationship with Christ. We act in the person of Christ. Celibacy is a sacrifice, but isn't that what Christianity is about? Christianity is about giving your life, not about receiving.

Those who think celibacy is the reason for the lack of vocations are mistaken. As we look into the future, we need to have a renewal of the priesthood. The church has renewed the liturgy in Vatican II. They renewed Holy Week. In Vatican I, the church renewed papal authority and infallibility. The church needs to have a council that renews the priesthood. This is an international problem. The more I travel with my television show and meet priests throughout the world, the more I realize the problems and difficulties are the same.

The Catholic church stinks when it comes to marketing the priesthood! The church is not media savvy, and this is a media world. We have this incredible treasure. We've got the Eucharist, we've got the Our Lady, and we've got the church, but we don't know how to get them out there. We stink at selling the most precious

> The church needs to review how much they are investing in, renewing, and strengthening our priests.

things we have! There are some religions that send their ministers away for two weeks and they get a certificate. But these guys have enthusiasm and they eat up the world. We tend to be very passive about our evangelization efforts. When I hear the pope speak about the new evangelization, new in its fervor, new in its message, I recognize that's what we have to do. We have to send the message of Christ, which is the same message as always. We have to send it to the world with enthusiasm and conviction. Unfortunately, if a priest makes a mistake, the entire image of the priesthood is damaged. Priests are people, too. We're human beings. We make mistakes like everyone else. It's not acceptable that because of isolated incidents, a shadow is cast on the entire priesthood. The church needs to review how much they are investing in, renewing, and strengthening our priests. We need to start marketing the priesthood!

> One of the things that I'd like to accomplish is I'd like to get the church back into the mainstream of life.

Bishops are more concerned about being CEOs than about being spiritual fathers. It's already starting to catch up with us. If fund-raising is the bishop's greatest responsibility and if fund-raising is the pastor's greatest responsibility, it's going to affect us spiritually. Part of the problem that we have today is that very few bishops really know their priests. The bigger the diocese, the less they know them. There's a huge concern in the church today with fund-raising for the future, having renovated churches, and securing endowments. I wonder if the church puts as much energy into the spiritual development, growth, and health of the entire people of God?

One of the things that I'd like to accomplish is to get the church back into the mainstream of life. We need to have a presence. We have a message that no one else has. It's the Gospel. It's two thousand years old and it not only teaches the truth about God, it teaches the truth about man. We can't be afraid of cameras, microphones, and computers. We have to use everything we have to communicate the Gospel. If Jesus

44

were here today, he'd probably be a talk show host. Because of the media world that we live in, it's a natural way to communicate with people in the way that they understand.

On any given Sunday, I can stand at my pulpit and I can preach to one thousand parishioners. But when I go on that camera I can reach anywhere between three and five million people. Not only is my show seen everywhere in Latin America, it is seen in most places where Hispanics reside. Unfortunately, I can only reach Cuba in a limited way. I understand that some of my videotapes have been smuggled into the country. Apparently, people will share and trade videotapes of shows that are seen in Miami. It's sad, but that's the only way they can have access to information.

I'm blessed, because television and radio have given me an opportunity to minister and to extend my hand to people as far as I can go. It's like a super-stretch priest. I receive E-mails from priests, nuns, laypeople, and even atheists. It's been such a surprise because I never expected to be on television, much less international television. I could not have imagined how popular the show has become. My motivation has nothing to do with self-interest, it has to do with bringing Christ to the people. It is such a humbling experience! But it's good to be able to reach out and help people, and guide them.

In Latin America, the church is central. It's very important. They don't have the extremely secularized society that we have in the states. It is much more a part of their culture than it is for us. There is an incredible affirmation from people. They want to know what priests have to say. I am convinced that priests, in a way, have distanced themselves from society. Society is really crying out for us. It is evident with the amount of self-help books available in the bookstore. It is also evident in the fact that there are a great deal of spiritual movements that seem to be going nowhere. It's a New Age thing.

45

Meditation—what do they meditate on? I believe they're looking for Christ, but they don't know it. It's our job as Catholics, and Christians, to take them there!

There is a priest in Brazil, Father Marcello Rossi, who has a unique way of bringing Catholics back to the church. He has a rock star presence. He's sold millions of CDs. I've had Marcello on my show twice. He's an amazingly humble and down-to-earth kind of guy who can can draw thousands of people to Mass at one time. Millions of people have returned to the church because of Father Rossi. What he has done for the church in Brazil, no bishop has been able to do. His Mass is like a rock concert. It's all marketing. Father Rossi has a different way of celebrating Mass and marketing the Catholic church, and it works.

> There is no doubt that God wrote this script for me. I didn't choose to do this.

The Hispanic community is in greatest need as far as identifying priests that they can relate to. I think Hispanics can relate to Father Rossi and me because we're just regular guys. The diocesan priest, your typical parish priest, has to be an outgoing person. As an extrovert, I can reach many people. When I'm more approachable, people feel they can talk to me more. I really believe that the reason the priesthood suited me, from the beginning of my vocation, through the whole discernment process and seminary years, is because I love God and I love his people. You have to be able to share life with people.

There is no doubt that God wrote this script for me. I didn't choose to do this. This must have been God's idea, because I know it wasn't mine! In spite of the success of my show, I try to keep very low-key and in check. I have a spiritual director and I go to confession every two weeks. I try to have a strong prayer life and I will _never, ever_ miss Mass. I can't go a day without Mass, even if I have to say it privately. I do not tape a television show without first saying Mass. There have been some very good older priests who have had a wonderful influence on me and have made an impact on my life. Their spirituality and the way they look at life has rubbed off on me. I try to remind people, I'm not the television priest. I'm the priest on television. There is a difference.

Hispanic Catholics are very respectful of the church and its authority. Dissent is not a Hispanic thing. Hispanics are profoundly Catholic, even the ones who don't go to church. I've been asked many times if the pope approves of my show. It's very important to the Latin American audience that the pope approves. Archbishop John P. Foley, who is the president of the Pontifical Council for Social Communications, assured me that the pope not only approves of my show, but has actually seen the show himself. That was amazing to hear. The pope is very interested in everything that has to do with the media, both positive and negative. The show looks like something that is very progressive. It's funny that a traditional person like myself ended up doing it. If a liberal priest ended up doing it, the show would probably be very different. I happen to be 100 percent orthodox and believe in the church's teaching.

I met the pope in 1996, a year after I was ordained. Bishop Harry J. Flynn, Archbishop of Saint Paul, Minnesota, invited a group of priests from the archdiocese of Miami to go to Rome. It was beautiful because I was able to assist at the papal altar at the feast of Saint Peter and Paul. I was able to meet His Holiness in a private audience the following day. It was just amazing. The archbishop presented me as Father Albert of the archdiocese of Miami. Because the pope has his doctorate in Spanish and actually speaks better Spanish than English, I told him in Spanish that I was Cuban American. He said, "Oh really? I pray for Cuba every day." My mother still keeps the picture of the pope and me in her dining room.

I was also able to meet the pope on World Youth Day in Paris, and then again on World Youth Day in Rome. I've been really blessed with all the times I've been in his presence.

I realized at a young age that God would have a very prominent place in my heart. I knew I could do many other things in my life, but serving God would be the only thing that could truly fulfill me as a man and as a human being. God became the most important thing in my life. Not only do I have a deep love for God, I have a deep love for his people. Those two points alone should be a requirement for the priesthood. The more I review my vocation and the more I pray about it, it makes perfect sense that I was led to be a priest.

If someone senses that God is calling you and tapping you on the shoulder, you begin to feel pulled by the desire to serve and belong to God. My pull has developed in many ways. What I felt at fifteen years old is not what I felt at twenty-five or even thirty. Life needs to develop. Priests, like any person, can go through a midlife crisis, or can say, "What if?" I've never had one regret about becoming a priest. In the end, if it's what God wants, the priesthood really isn't a choice.

2

"Do you want me to come down to that rectory and tell people what you're really like?"

The Celibate Life

Have YOU EVER paused and reflected about life in the rectory? Should the church lift the ban on celibacy and allow priests to marry? What does a priest do when he's not working? Do you think a Catholic priest is any different as a person?

THROUGHOUT the three years I've spent putting this book together, I have been told countless stories about priests' lives. Trust me, life in the rectory reaches far beyond a couple of priests sharing living quarters. The rectory is a paradox of sorts. These grown men may not always get along, but they are assigned to live with each other, and eat, work, relax, and pray together.

On Palm Sunday of 2001, I was scheduled to lector at our 8:00 A.M. Liturgy. As I was in the sacristy preparing for Mass, our pastor, Father Michael, walked in and asked, "So, how's the book coming along?"

"Not bad," I told him. "But I'm having some difficulty with the chapter on celibacy."

"I don't want to hear it," he jokingly snapped. "You think you're having difficulty writing that chapter, think about us priests!"

Everyone in the sacristy began to laugh at his remarks. But I suddenly realized how right he was.

While celibacy is cited as one of the principle reasons for the lack of vocations, the notion of socializing with their priest is an equally foreign concept to many people. Like everyone else who works all week, priests enjoy their day off and dining out, the camaraderie of friends, the arts, and even the occasional pranks. In this respect, they're no different than the rest of us, as you'll see in this chapter.

EARLY IN THE 1980s, when it was customary for the pastor to be "the boss," very conservative and very strict, the curate had to get permission from him to come and go, as well as indicate the time element for each outing. The curate was not allowed to leave the rectory on a Saturday or Sunday, unless with the pastor.

Having come not so long before from another continent, I was not yet fully familiar with rectory regulations. One Saturday evening I left the rectory after an evening Mass. It was January and freezing cold! When I returned, I was dismayed to discover I had been "locked out." The slide bolt had been pulled from inside so my key was useless.

I rang the doorbell and pounded on the door in an attempt to awaken the pastor. Nothing worked! Finally, I was forced to walk to a public telephone to call the pastor. He did not answer the phone. A freezing rain had started to fall.

Finally, I dialed 911. The pastor was very elderly and I thought maybe he had died. In a few minutes, police and fire apparatus arrived. They raised their ladder to his window. The pastor sat up in his bed and demanded, "What the hell is going on?"

I never did become one of his favorite people.

† Father Joseph Parel
Archdiocese of Hartford

IN THE OLDEN DAYS, pastors could be cruel to their assistants. One would think that since assistants ranged from the ages of twenty-five to fifty they would have the status of junior executives. Instead, most of them were treated like lowly assistants, having to adhere to rules such as having a nine o'clock curfew.

One assistant enjoyed a snack of milk and cookies before going to bed until the pastor decided to put an end to these evening treats by padlocking the refrigerator.

Another time when an assistant stopped at the pastor's office to inform him that he would be at the hospital visiting a priest classmate, the pastor said, "He is not a member of this parish. Go back to your room."

We had one priest, Father Peter, who was always playing practical jokes on everyone. One day he came to our rectory for a visit. I had just returned from the parish hall where the kids were planning their youth dance. I noticed Father Peter's new white car parked at the parish hall and figured this would be a good time to get him back.

As I entered the rectory where some other priests had gathered, I exclaimed, "I just gave those kids a hard scolding!"

Father Peter responded, "Leave those kids alone."

"But they were throwing stones at the shiny new Buick in front of the hall."

Well, Father Peter leaped from his chair and ran outside. The rest of the priests in the rectory began to laugh out loud because they knew that I had baited him.

† Father A. J. Fisher
Archdiocese of Anchorage

†

IT'S IMPORTANT to note that I have a rather strong voice. As Judge Harry Kramer said many years ago, "Father, you're loud."

It was a very hot summer night. I had all the windows open in my rooms. At 3:30 A.M. Sunday morning, I heard a lot of boisterous laughter outside the rectory. I got up, looked out the window, and there in the rose bed fronting Fifth Avenue were three young college boys, obviously quite drunk, rolling around on the grass and in the bed of roses.

Obviously, I was upset. I had been wakened from a sound sleep and these fellows were damaging our precious rose bed. I went to the dark window and called out loudly, "All right you guys, GET MOVIN'!" Startled, the three got up and began looking around for the source of the deep voice.

Two of them quickly ran off. The third, however, stayed a moment longer. He bowed profoundly toward the Cathedral Rectory and said, "Thank you, God." Then he ran off, too.

† Father Leo V. Vanyo
Diocese of Pittsburgh

$$\dagger$$

SOMETIMES my mom threatens me: "Do you want me to come down to that rectory and tell people what you're *really* like?"

† Father Larry J. Hess
Diocese of Allentown

$$\dagger$$

A BACKACHE can spoil a good night's sleep. That was my experience of nighttime rest for a good part of my life until I discovered the existence of the water bed.

Several friends had mentioned they owned a water bed and how comfortable they felt in it. Still, I wasn't sure I wanted to spend the money and then have to move the bed every time I was transferred. (And I was being transferred quite often at the time.)

One morning I woke up with an excruciating backache. That did it! I made up my mind to get a water bed. It took me another two weeks of reading about them and looking for a good bargain before I finally went out to buy one. The $150 price tag soon increased to over $300 before I had acquired the needed extras to go with it.

The store sent someone over to set it up. I watched carefully since I probably would have to take it apart and put it back together someday. When everything was in place and the water was being hosed into the vinyl mattress, the man from the store had to leave, saying, "I have another appointment. Just shut off the water when it's full. Everything should go well." He told me to stop the flow of the water when the mattress reached a certain height.

After I had shut off the water, I noticed pleats in the vinyl mattress. No matter how hard I tried to smooth them off, they kept coming back. I hadn't been warned about that. Leaning

53

over the mattress, I pulled at one end and tugged here and there. Nothing. I was getting quite frustrated. My back was starting to ache. I hadn't realized how heavy a water mattress could be.

Just at that moment, I heard our cook's excited voice over the intercom. "Father, come down quickly, there's water dripping into the pastor's office."

"Oh, no!" I exclaimed. "That's all I need!" The pastor's office was directly underneath my bedroom. I quickly looked around the water bed to see where the water might be leaking out. Everything was dry. Perhaps the mattress was leaking in the middle from beneath the bed. Could it be that the liner was faulty, too?

I rushed downstairs and ran into the pastor's office, expecting the worst. Everything looked normal and dry. That's when I realized someone was up to something. I walked into the kitchen and found what I was looking for.

The cook and the housekeeper were giggling away. They immediately saw I wasn't smiling. I remember saying to them in a very harsh and threatening tone, "Don't you realize you broadcast your joke all over the rectory and even into the office? It's not funny!" I turned around and walked back upstairs. They tell me there was fire coming out of my eyes!

Once in my room, I let myself fall on my water bed and floated for a while, thinking about what had just taken place. I had to admit to myself they had caught me off guard. It was a good trick and a funny one at that. I laughed so hard that I bounced up and down on the water bed for some five minutes. I never told them that, until now.

The moral of this story: It's good to laugh at ourselves. Especially in rectories!

† Father Roger P. Chabot
Diocese of Portland, ME

✝

WHEN YOU LIVE in the rectory, you have to be prepared for anything. Once, I woke up at 5:30 A.M. and couldn't get back to sleep. I knew something was wrong, but what? My instinct was strong but not well defined. Well, once I got over to the church, I knew what was wrong.

The boiler had gone off and would not run for anything. The first call for "service" went in at 7:20 A.M., the second call at 7:45 A.M., and the third call at 8:15 A.M. In between, the organist called to report that her car would not start. The fourth call went in to the manager of the service company at 9:00 A.M.

As I was getting "hotter" by the second, the church was getting colder. The repairman finally arrived at 10:35 A.M. to tell us we were out of oil. Odd, I thought. Saint Patrick's (the church down the street) was out of oil this morning, and so were we. The regular delivery had not been made during the week.

Could it have had anything to do with the price increase of a few days earlier?

The oil truck arrived at 11:35 A.M. It left 1,768 gallons at the church, 777 gallons at the school, and 649 gallons at the convent, for a total of 3,194 gallons at $1.10 per gallon.

✝ *Father Charles E. Maher*
Diocese of Providence

✝

THE ONE THING that always comes into the mind of people considering the priesthood is the word "celibacy."

"How do you handle celibacy?" was invariably the question I would hear.

In 1973 when I was considering the priesthood, I told my spiritual director that I was thinking about the priesthood, but in no way was I thinking about celibacy.

He told me, "Well, don't come seeking the priesthood until you have a desire for celibacy so strong that it becomes a gift. And it is something you want to embrace, not something you have to embrace." So I did!

I can remember taking a "private promise" of celibacy. Just to try it out. To see what it was like. I really needed to be free from the whole dating scene. I used to be so caught up with dating. There was a time that if I didn't have two or three dates a weekend I thought something was wrong.

It wasn't so much that I was choosing to date, it was something that I had to do. It was as if I was possessed by it. It was a hangover from my past life. So I remember trying it (the private promise) and I thought, "My God, this is great!"

I can relate to brothers and sisters without the thought of "hitting" on each other. I can have a basic conversation without thinking, "What is this leading to?"

It actually happened one time. A friend of mine asked me to watch him play hockey. I put on my jacket and hat and went to watch him. I had my clerics on underneath, but I was zipped up because the hockey rink was so cold. As I arrived at the rink my friend told me to sit with his girlfriend and pointed toward the bleachers.

So I went and sat by his girlfriend. Within two minutes she got up and walked to the other bleachers. I was thinking, "What's going on?" My friend told me later that she thought I was trying to pick her up. He never told her that "the priest" was going to sit beside her. I said thanks a lot!

I can remember being free to share and look beyond evaluating somebody that I was with. I began to look at the other gender as a "sister" in the Lord, a person who has needs and who I don't need to date. But who I can love in community in Christ!

I found a great freedom and liked it so much that I eventually made it permanent.

† Father Larry J. Hess
Diocese of Allentown

IN MY HEART, I believe that the church would be better if there wasn't mandatory celibacy. That way, a priest could choose.

Anonymous

WHEN PEOPLE ASK ME about celibacy, I try to relate a very practical story about my mother. My mother had a mini stroke in 1977 and then developed Alzheimer's. She lost her sight and had to be fed through a tube. She was in and out of the hospital four to five times a year. At my own expense, I had to provide home nurses to care for her during the day.

My brother, who is also a priest, shared the duties of taking care of our mother. At 11:00 P.M. every night, after being at the parish all day, I would pack a bag and run home to be with my mother. My brother and I switched back and forth each day.

Up until the time she got sick, my complete attention and my heart and soul were with the rectory and church. After she got sick, every time the phone rang in the rectory, I would jump. It was usually an emergency call from my mom.

I then saw the wisdom of the church in very graphic terms. You can't have one eye in one place and one eye in the other, or one ear in one place and one ear in the other. You just can't do it!

57

To me, to be a priest and a family man, with the demands of fatherhood, children, and wife, it just cannot be done. You can't do both. At least not correctly, anyway.

† Monsignor Joseph J. Granato
Archdiocese of Newark

I WOULD SAY that celibacy is the overwhelming concern of young men that I speak with. The question of whether or not they could lead a celibate life is always on their mind. I'm very honest with the people I speak with. I tell them that a celibate life can be a difficult sacrifice at times, but it's one that is necessary.

As a priest, you try to live in imitation of Jesus and to represent him. Jesus wasn't married. The goal of a priest is to remain open at every moment; to be able to serve the people who trust in your care and not have a heart divided.

Priests also have to be careful. I think a lot of women are looking for a man who understands them and listens and cares for them. Many guys tend to be oblivious to their wife's needs. Priests can be very good listeners as well as caring, gentle, and sensitive. Women can see these qualities in priests and there are times when they will be attracted to the priest who is offering his help.

† Father Michael A. Caridi
Diocese of Pittsburgh

AS BAPTIZED CHRISTIANS, all of us are called to be aware of and reflect on the gift of our own sexuality. This is an integral part of our dignity as created in the image of God and claimed for Christ. Chastity is a component of the Christian lifestyle and often stands in contradiction to the values of the world. Understanding and accepting the gift of who I am from God and its dynamic within the context of a marital relationship is critical to the Christian lifestyle.

When one chooses celibacy, it is a fundamental choice for chastity. The lifestyle which emerges should never, at least in the context of men, be one of the eccentric bachelor. This choice can never be rooted in an aversion to the gift of one's sexuality nor can it be an escape from what is construed as sin. The choice is Kingdom-oriented, as is marriage. Each speaks of the dynamic of the Kingdom of God: marriage as a sign in the here and now as the Kingdom unfolds; chastity as a sign of the Kingdom to come when Christ returns in glory. The issue, of course, is whether this sign is rooted to priesthood in and of itself. This has been and will continue to be a question over which the church prays and reflects. Guided by the Spirit, the Body of Christ continues to maintain this to be so.

Personally, I think the danger is to miss the larger context in which chastity and celibacy fit within the design of the church and spend too much energy placing it within the confines of the priesthood, at the expense of the greater picture of the Kingdom.

† Anonymous

FOUR OF US PRIESTS were playing golf one day, and after golf we went out for dinner. Before the end of the dinner the waitress handed us the check and said, "If I do not give you the check now, you will have to pay an added cabaret tax as the music and dancing begins at 9:00 P.M., unless you guys are with the F.B.I. (then she whispered) or priests!"

One of us asked her how she knew we were priests. She said, without hesitation, "None of you are wearing a wedding ring or a college ring, and no wives would let you guys dress like that. It's the most uncoordinated attire that I've seen in a long time!"

† Father John F. Reardon
Archdiocese of New York

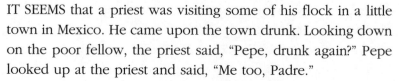

IT SEEMS that a priest was visiting some of his flock in a little town in Mexico. He came upon the town drunk. Looking down on the poor fellow, the priest said, "Pepe, drunk again?" Pepe looked up at the priest and said, "Me too, Padre."

† Father Victor Seidel, S.T.S.
Diocese of Savannah

I AM VERY DIFFICULT to live with. I like things my way, whether it be which lights are left on or turned off, or what the refrigerator looks like. God has done well in not allowing me to be married. I've made several mistakes in the rectory. The gist of some of my confessions includes these mistakes. I find it very difficult to live with someone who has a different lifestyle than me.

† Father Joseph A. Rulli
Diocese of South Bend

OFTEN WHEN TALKING to engaged couples about accepting each other as they are, with all their faults and foibles, I relate to them an experience that I find humorous to this day.

I had an assistant about a year and a half older than me. We were truly the "Odd Couple." I was Oscar and he was Felix. I smoked, cussed when necessary, had a cluttered desk, and didn't worry much about how the rectory looked.

He, on the other hand, didn't smoke, didn't cuss, and his desk was always neat and clean. He was constantly emptying the ashtrays, picking the newspaper up off the floor and putting it back together in the proper order.

I would put my dirty dishes in the dishwasher and he would take them out and put them back in the way he thought they should be. He would put all the spices in alphabetical order and keep the refrigerator neat and tidy with everything where it should be.

At 2:00 P.M. on a Saturday afternoon he would go to the sacristy and get the water and wine ready for the 5:00 P.M. Mass. Despite our many differences, we got along well and accepted each other the way we were. We would go to the racetrack together once a month for a night out and often went together to a parishioner's house for a meal.

I guess we had the ideal relationship. I have lived in other parishes with other priests where I had great difficulty being charitable.

† Father Ray Hofmann
Archdiocese of Louisville

A FEW YEARS AGO, several priests and I were sitting down to eat lunch after having played eighteen holes of golf. One of the priests announced that he had been given a new assignment. When he told us the name of the parish, we started teasing him because it was one of the smallest parishes in the diocese with only ninety-two families altogether.

With so much emphasis being placed on evangelization and bringing back the unchurched, we asked what he was planning to do. His response, "By Christmas, I'll have the parish trimmed down to a workable seventy-five families!"

We all just about rolled on the floor with laughter.

† Father John C. Vojtek
Diocese of Pittsburgh

> "The people of my parish are
> what fulfill me most as a priest."

Joseph A. Daley

Ordained IN 1968 to a small religious order called the Pallottine Fathers, he is currently pastor of Saint Anthony of Padua church in Cody, Wyoming. To say that Saint Anthony's is a rural parish is akin to calling the pope "just another priest." Saint Anthony's alone covers an area that includes Yellowstone National Park and stretches into three states. It is the largest parish in the lower forty-eight states covering over seventy-six hundred square miles.

IN ADDITION to this awesome responsibility, Father Daley is very much involved with the youth of today. He is central to

a parish youth program unlike any other in the country.
Going on its eighth year, the students in Father Daley's parish
go to Rome on a semiannual basis as a regular part of their
religious education process.

After spending a great deal of time on the East Coast,
Father Daley gives us a new perspective when comparing the
Catholic church in the American west versus the Catholic
church in the eastern states.

Profile

AS PECULIAR as it may sound, I can't give a specific reason for why I became a priest. My vocation was just kind of "there." But upon reflection, I see that the foundation was laid during my grade school years. My mom and dad talked about it, the nuns talked about it in school; it was just the topic of conversation. In many Irish families, the oldest child, be it a boy or girl, went to the convent or the seminary. In those days, if a son went to the seminary, it brought a lot of respect to the family. That's not the case today, but that's the way it was in the 1950s. It was normal that vocations were a high probability.

When I entered the seminary in 1959 I had certain expectations of the priesthood, but that all changed. Right in the middle of that experience, the Second Vatican Council occurred and the role of the priest and the church began to transform. Vatican II brought about different roles and functions for priests and different notions of obedience and superiors. Things were changing.

Prior to being ordained, on the very last day of school, our morality professor walked in and said, "I just want to give you a message. You guys are going to be ordained with questions. Because of Vatican II, you're the first class ordained with no answers. Go do it, boys, there's an adventure out there!" Before

Vatican II the church had an answer for everything: just follow the rules and obey canon law. We were ordained with many questions, so it ended up that we didn't have expectations.

I was ordained in 1968. Nationwide, the ordination class of 1968 is considered the last big class in any diocese. In my class alone we had roughly eighty or ninety priests who were ordained. Now, a diocese is considered lucky if it has ten.

> In my class alone we had roughly eighty or ninety priests who were ordained. Now, a diocese is considered lucky if it has ten.

When I left the seminary, I didn't know what was going to happen. My other classmates felt the same way. We knew the old church. Everything was set by rules and there were very few meetings, etc. Before Vatican II, there was no such thing as a parish center. Lectors, girl altar servers, and parish councils didn't exist. Vatican II was all experimentation. There was a "try this and try that and let's see if it works" attitude. Communion services, lay leaders, concelebrated Masses, and Masses said in English were all brand new. When I was ordained, the Mass was said half in English, and half in Latin. Within a year, the Mass was all English. The deacons at that time sat in the pew. There was no place for a deacon up on the altar. A lot of what we did was with our bishop, a kind of "hunt and peck" thing. Laypeople were bent out of shape, too. There were many changes that I never anticipated, but it was all exciting and very dynamic.

Although I never questioned my vocation, I wouldn't call my seminary experience enjoyable. It was very strict and very conservative. Today, when I tell seminarians or any students about life in the old seminary, they think I'm making it up. After you wrote a letter you had to leave the envelope open so the superior could read it. If he didn't like something he read, he blacked it out. When we received mail, it was already opened and read before we had an opportunity to read it. We were only allowed to walk in groups of three, and parents could visit only once a month. Since I was a religious at the time, I couldn't have a summer job and was not permitted to go home. Seminarians today wouldn't put up with those rules for a minute. Society was different in the '50s. You respected the police and people in authority. You questioned nothing. Even though the atmosphere was very strict, it was viewed as normal. We weren't upset by the rules; it was just the way it was.

Although the times were very strict, we did have a great deal of fun. And, occasionally, we broke the rules. One thing we tried to do in those days was outwit the nuns. When I went to grade school, all the nuns carried "clickers." When Sister would click it, you knew what to do: either kneel, genuflect, or stand up. When Sister clicked that thing you just did what you were supposed to do. I went to an all-boys' high school, and if you looked at the priests the wrong way they'd kick you in the rear end or they'd just plain deck you!

I was ordained to a very small religious community called the Pallottine Fathers. Today, there are not many priests left in the country that belong to the community. The Pallottines had five parishes and a brand-new high school in South Jersey. In my first assignment I was sent to teach high school. Pallottines, like many other priests, are not given a choice of assignments. I taught American history and religion from 1968 to 1971. Later, I received my master's degree in American history. My first week on the job was normal, but then again, it was new. Thankfully, the kids at that time were still fairly obedient.

I've had many assignments in my thirty-three years of ministry. Before being sent to the "Wild West" in various pastorate positions, I was assigned to the University of Maryland Medical Center-Institute for Emergency Medicine. It was the first shock trauma center in the world. Without question, the sights of any trauma center can give the most seasoned physician pause. Though horrific accidents and medical emergencies were commonplace, it was a young boy, who passed away peacefully in the middle of the night, and his funeral, that has remained with me throughout the years.

I happened to be in the hospital at around 3:00 A.M. getting ready to go home when my beeper sounded. I was notified by the hospital staff that a young boy had just died of leukemia. I spent time with the young mother and father and asked them what I could do for them. I asked them if I could contact their reverend and they said to me, "Father, we don't have one; would you bury our boy?" I told them I would.

After a beautiful service, what I found to be most poignant was that they buried the little boy in an old Black slave cemetery in Baltimore. Apparently, it is still available for funerals today. The boy's father and uncle actually hand-dug the grave. To hear the family singing hymns while gathered around the grave was very emotional. The boy's father then climbed down into the freshly dug grave and the mother handed the father the casket. The father gently laid his son to rest. As the

This one church covers over 7,600 square miles and three states including Yellowstone National Park.

family continued to sing, the father and uncle began to slowly fill the grave with dirt using only shovels. It was the most memorable and spiritually moving event that I have ever experienced.

When my Maryland Medical Center assignment ended, I was transferred out West and began serving as pastor in different churches. In 1993, I was directed by the bishop to a church in Cody, Wyoming. It was not just another parish. Saint Anthony of Padua happens to be the largest parish by area in the lower forty-eight states. This one church covers over seventy-six hundred square miles and three states including Yellowstone National Park. As if that isn't enough, the diocese of Cheyenne covers an area of over 97,000 square miles. This is also the largest diocese in the lower forty-eight states.

Summertime is tourist season in the Great West. Since a part of our parish covers Yellowstone National Park, there is a great influx of people. We get nothing but praise from tourists. When they find out how far the priest comes to say Mass while they're touring the park, they're very thankful. We actually have regular Sunday Mass at Old Faithful through the summer months. A priest in our parish will travel over 130 miles, one way, just to say Mass for the tourists and our regular parishioners. Typically, people attend our Mass from all over the world. Some write to us at Christmastime. Others send checks. It's an inspiration that the Masses are so well attended. Tourists who visit our church at Saint Anthony of Padua also praise our parish.

The bishop told me I was being sent to Saint Anthony for a specific reason. "Implement Vatican II," he ordered. The last pastor was a good man, but he was from the old school. He passed away after a battle with cancer. The parishioners were very open-minded to the change. It has taken eight years, but Vatican II is here. In that short amount of time we have practically rebuilt the entire church.

I've learned a great deal about the Catholic church in the western states versus the church in the eastern part of the country. Churches in the East are supposed to be avant-garde. Although some may be, the laypeople in the West have a different outlook on their churches. Westerners have a strong sense of "ownership" in their parish. Because of the vast and barren area that a parish covers, the parishioners of a western church understand that they must be "church-involved" for their church to flourish. They know that there are fewer parishioners, and the bishops are further away. They know that if they don't get involved they will have no church. Lay leadership has made an indelible mark on the universal church. I always try to instill in my parishioners their need to run the parish. They are going to be there long after I leave. The depth of lay leadership has clearly been one of my biggest surprises since being ordained.

The West and the western Catholic church has an entirely different outlook on life. One needs to look at the people and the society and how it functions as a community. Wyoming is one of the most republican states in the union. The people in Wyoming are not antidemocratic, they just want big brother out of their life. They have no time for Washington, D.C. That's the whole western attitude: "Leave us alone and we'll do fine."

> If you want to be on the cutting edge of society, . . . there is nothing better than the Catholic priesthood.

Similarly, if someone approaches me regarding a vocation, I handle it differently here than I would in the East. Clearly, it depends on the individual who is considering the priesthood as to what I will say. This holds true in any part of the country. But in the West, many of the kids here work on ranches and they don't have many opportunities to meet with a lot of people.

For some I might suggest they go to college and meet new people and experience life beyond the ranch or farm. For someone else I might say they're ready for the seminary tomorrow. Each person and each personality is handled differently.

In a general sense, and I've said this many times regarding vocations, if you want to be on the cutting edge of society, from politics, to moral issues, to legal and community issues, there is nothing better than the Catholic priesthood. If you like people and get along well with them, if you enjoy keeping active and have a great capacity to love, then the priesthood is the place to be.

One of the reasons for the lack of vocations today is the materialism of society. Parents say there's no money and no future in the priesthood. Kids today get flack if they talk about the seminary. The parents will look at them and ask, "You're kidding, right?" But, hopefully, that's beginning to shift. We used to get many second-career men like lawyers who quit their jobs to join the seminary. Now we're seeing a slight increase in the number of young men coming right out of high school and college who have expressed an interest in the priesthood. A change is coming.

As always, someone is bound to ask about not being married. I've found that they're not so much focused on "celibacy" as they are about the lack of a spouse. My role as a priest does provide me with freedoms. If a layperson is married, and if they're committed to their families (as they should be), then their world is restricted to spouse and kids. As an unmarried person, I have no limits like that. My schedule is more free. Although priests have a great deal of responsibilities, we don't have the commitments that a family man does. Our obligations are just different.

Ironically, I truly feel that God is with me when I work on annulment cases. For me to help a person realize that they are not a monster, and that they're not the worst person on the earth, is very rewarding. And it's not just when couples face the fact that they've had a bad marriage just like many other people. It's when they realize that they are worth something in God's eyes.

The people of my parish are what fulfill me most as a priest.

Any time people are confronted with a major decision and I can help them deal with it to the point where they are comfortable, I think the people feel, without ever using words, that somehow the Lord touched them or was walking with them. I do know the Lord works through me during such times.

God is also present with me every time I say Mass. There is nothing better than when a parishioner comments on how effectively I preached. Most of my homilies are derived from recent news events that happened through the week. I know this affects their lives. I also never use the words "me" and "you" in my homilies. I always use the word "we." I want my congregation to know that we're in this together. God's presence is always shining during a funeral Mass. For family and friends to say they find peace in what I say makes me feel that the Lord is somehow working through me to help them through their grief.

The people of my parish are what fulfill me most as a priest. Pope John Paul has directed his priests to "get out and do things, don't just keep the faith within the church walls. Get out there and take the faith to the community." He's opened up all kinds of avenues, and this is very evident in my parish, especially among the kids. The kids today care a lot about the pope.

The youth of today are an inspiration to me, especially the high school kids. Many people knock teenagers. Admittedly, until about five years ago, I knocked them too. Many kids are self-centered and egotistical. But that's changing. There is a new sense of service among teenagers today. Although many teens are focused on establishing good careers in the business world, they have not forgotten that they have responsibilities to society. Whether it's social or political issues, the poor or downtrodden, I've found that today's kids are very sensitive. They have a lot of challenges in school and life in general, and they seem to be more interested in vocations.

I know of no other parish in the country that sends its high school kids, juniors and seniors, to Rome for Holy Week as a regular part of their religious education. The kids work very hard to raise all the money. There are no fund-raisers, no begging for gifts, and no parents writing checks. The students finance the trip themselves. After the pope came to Denver for World Youth Day in 1993, the students wanted to go to the next World Youth Day scheduled for Manila. No way were we sending our kids to Manila. After many discussions, we decided to send them to Rome. The students have gone every other year since 1996.

Saint Anthony's is not heaven, but it's a wonderful place to be. I've come to find that God is also present in me through my laypeople. I offer them a challenge and they go searching. I think our prayer life has deepened. They're not perfect people, as none of us are. They know they're on a journey and they know that their journey is unique. I tell them all the time, "When I meet the Lord, he's not going to ask me, 'How big was your parish, how much money did you make, and what did the church look like?' He's going to ask me, 'Did you teach the people?'" I'm not on a quest to be popular. I'm on a quest to help people find their own way to the Lord. There's no better way to do that than through the priesthood.

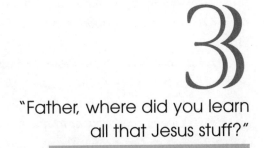

"Father, where did you learn all that Jesus stuff?"

A Funny Thing Happened

Can YOU IMAGINE the questions young kids ask their priests? Can you imagine walking into your manager's office tomorrow and taking a vow of obedience to him?

WITH OVER two million kids attending Catholic schools and another four million enrolled in religious education programs, I knew that priests would be submitting great questions and comments uttered by children. Because of their unique ability to view the world without bias, their thoughts are precious and pure, as you'll see in some of the following stories. And priests aren't reluctant to tell about the times they've been caught off guard.

And it's not just children that can catch a priest off guard. So can bishops and cardinals. Although the topic of the hierarchy was included in my initial letter, I was convinced that priests would be hesitant to speak about their superiors in a forum such as this for fear of reprimand or just plain having their words misconstrued. Thankfully, I was mistaken.

The anecdotes throughout this book are meant simply to show that priests are people, too. Well, so are bishops, cardinals, and the pope, as I'm sure you'll agree.

ONE DAY the kindergarten class was in line to get their lunches. When I went over, one of the boys in line asked, "Father, where did you learn all of that Jesus stuff?"

† Father Henry C. Vavasseur
Diocese of Baton Rouge

IT WAS THE end of the first day of school and a new first-grader entered Sister's office. We both looked at him and asked if anything was wrong. As he began to answer, his eyes welled up with tears and his lower lip trembled.

I bent down near him and asked again what was wrong. He managed to tell me that he didn't know which bus to take.

I brought him to the window and we looked at a school yard filled with buses.

I said to him, "Oh, that's easy, just take the yellow bus!" The little boy just looked at me, then looked at the buses and began to laugh. We quickly found his bus and he was off.

Another problem solved in the life of a parish priest!

† Monsignor Gerardo J. Colacicco
Archdiocese of New York

DURING ONE TEACHING ASSIGNMENT, I had a class which was a handful to control. I made one particularly troublesome student sit next to my desk all the time. One day I arrived at class a little late. The problem child was in his place next to my desk.

I walked in the room, never taking my eyes off the class, put my papers on the desk, and sat down. But the chair wasn't there, and I landed on the floor.

As a little giggle passed through the class, I hopped up and grabbed the kid next to my desk. He loudly proclaimed his innocence. I firmly seated him back at his desk and went on to teach. The student was tossed out of school a month later.

A couple of years ago, I was honored by the police department of a neighboring town for helping catch a criminal who had fled into Newark. At the same ceremony, the student I had chastised was also being honored as a hero cop. We had a warm reunion!

I also had a pet parakeet that would come to school with me once in a while. It was a neat little bird that rode around on my shoulder and jabbered away. It would pick up all sorts of words and expressions, sometimes at first hearing.

One day, the bird was in the faculty lounge with me. A teacher came in, quite upset, sat down, and said "Son of a bitch!" Then he went on to tell me about how frustrated he was with his last class.

After that, I left the lounge and went up to my class with the bird still on my shoulder. (The bird was an occasional visitor to class and enjoyed flying around and dropping in on students).

When I came into class, the parakeet flew to a kid who was sitting at his desk, landed on his head, and loudly and clearly said, "Son of a bitch!" The kid looked at me and said, "Did you hear that?"

I said to him, "Yes, even the bird knows!"

† Father Philip J. Waters, O.S.B.
Archdiocese of Newark

MY FOUR-YEAR-OLD NEPHEW Peter was alone in the front pew of a convent chapel as I was celebrating a weekday Mass at Loretta Convent in Mullingar, Ireland.

Peter never moved a muscle all through the Mass. He never stood, and never sat. He just kneeled there with the top of his blond head showing above the pew.

That is, until after the period of prayer after Communion. I stood up, went to the altar, and said, "Let us pray." That's when Peter moved for the first time, stuck his head up, and said: "Who's stoppin' you?"

† Father James R. Wilson
Diocese of Boise

✝

I AM A NONSMOKER. I have been told that nicotine stains are not uncommon for heavy cigarette smokers. At Mass, when the priest washes his hands, having handled and prepared the Offertory Gifts, he quietly says: "Lord, wash away my iniquity; cleanse me from my sins."

Imagine my surprise and amusement while doing a question and answer session with the the third grade religion class when sweet little Megan asked: "Father Jim, when you're washing your hands, why do you say, 'Lord, wash away my "nicotine" and cleanse me from my sins?'"

Kind of makes a priest wonder what exactly the folks in the pews hear when he preaches a homily.

✝ Father James B. Braaten
Diocese of Bismarck

✝

I WAS AT A SCHOOL with the National Dominican nuns. There were three sets of alarm bells at the school: one for fire, one for a tornado, and one for an earthquake.

One day the alarm bells went off. I grabbed all the kids and told them to hustle out of the building and get to the football field.

As I started taking roll call, two of the kids were talking and I asked them what they were saying. The kids informed me that the reason no one else was on the football field was because it was the tornado alarm that went off.

I told the kids to keep their mouths shut and to hustle back inside. Upon arriving inside, I was greeted by the nuns. They reprimanded me, "Good job, Father, you could have killed them if it was a real tornado!"

† Father Carl J. Hood
Diocese of Memphis

WHEN I WAS A YOUNG PRIEST and principal of a high school, I rode the buses with the students and teams to away games. One Sunday afternoon, as we were returning from a victory, I told the bus driver to pull into the next highway restaurant so that we could all get something to eat.

The bus driver and I sat at a side table and enjoyed a chicken dinner. When the waitress brought the bill, I noticed she charged for only one dinner. The bus driver reached for his wallet and said it was the Roman collar that got a free meal. I signaled the waitress and asked if she made a mistake charging for only one meal.

"Oh no," she said, "we never charge bus drivers."

† Father Thomas J. Peterman, V.F.
Diocese of Wilmington

THERE IS a local school in our area that asks pastors to help fill the need for substitute teachers. Many teachers were attending a workshop one day and a student said, "They should call it Holy Week. We had three pastors in one day!"

On another occasion, the eighth-graders came into the classroom and I overheard one student say to the other, "It's the priest. Does he know any math?"

I do, in fact, know math, having majored in math in college. So, unflustered, I sat the students down and immediately asked, "What's the fourth book in the Bible?"

A lone student's hand went up. "Numbers," he said.

"You bet," I responded, "and I know my 'numbers' very well! Furthermore, I was reading my Bible this very morning and it said the people were spellbound because Jesus taught with 'authority' and not like the scribes."

I approached a student in the front row and looked intently down at him, and continued, "Today, I'm teaching with authority!"

† Father Jim D. Friedrich
Diocese of Sioux Falls

WHEN I WAS a catechist preparing young people for confirmation, the pastor of a neighboring church invited me to have dinner with the bishop (not the bishop of my diocese). After dinner, the bishop excused himself and went to use the men's room.

Shortly thereafter, I followed.

While the bishop was in the men's room, he had bent over to tie his shoe. I had no idea that he was tying his shoe. I proceeded to walk in, and as I pushed the door open, I slammed the bishop in his rear end, sending him flying headfirst into the wall.

He recovered, and the liturgy began. At communion I went to the tabernacle. I was taking a ciborium to the altar, and I tripped up the steps, sending hosts in all directions. I muttered an expletive which all the kids sitting in the front row heard.

79

Later, the bishop pulled me aside and asked me what diocese I was studying for. I told him, and he responded, "I'll pray for your bishop!"

† Father Edward R. Schleicher
Diocese of Pittsburgh

†

IN 1990, I was sent to the North American College in Rome for its three-month continuing education program for priests. It was truly a unique privilege. Saint Peter's is a ten-minute downhill walk from where I lived. It was twenty minutes, uphill, on the way home.

The North American College is also home-away-from-home for U.S. bishops when they take part in a meeting at the Vatican.

One morning at breakfast, one of my confreres, who is definitely not a "morning person," was joined by a middle-aged, balding man.

The man sat down next to my friend and said, "Hi, I'm Joe Bernardin."

The priest said, "Hi Joe! Where ya from?"

"Chicago," came the answer.

It took several seconds for the priest to finally realize, "Oh, it's *that* Joe Bernardin," and began to apologize profusely to his Eminence.

Cardinal Bernardin explained that no apology was necessary. Instead, the conversation had given the cardinal a good laugh to begin his day.

† Father Thomas J. Extejt
Diocese of Toledo

†

MY MOM was active in the archdiocese for a number of years and was a very good Catholic. As she got older, she started to develop Alzheimer's. In 1993, Mom was having difficulty getting around. Occasionally, she would ask the caregiver to drop her off at the rectory. To keep her busy, I would give her little chores to do. Paperwork, organizing, things of that nature. She was thrilled to keep active.

One particular day I was very busy. I had three different Masses to celebrate. The first Mass I had was for the school children. There were about three hundred kids in attendance and my mother sat right there with the kids. Even though she was seventy-five years old, she loved being a part of the dialogue homily with the children.

I then had a Mass to celebrate at Trinity College. My mom had actually taught classes at Trinity years before. When we got there, she was a hit. The students knew her, and the Sisters remembered her. She had a good time. After Mass we went to get lunch.

The last Mass I celebrated that day was at the Lakeview Nursing Home. I was using a dialogue homily to get the residents involved with the service. My mom was sitting right in the front seat. For the first two questions I asked, my mom raised her hand and answered them properly. When I asked the third question, my mom again answered correctly. I was thinking, "Boy, this is bad, Mom is answering all the questions. There are forty other people in the room. How can I get the other residents involved with this process?"

When I asked other questions, I began to ignore my mom on purpose. I called on "Ann" and asked her what she thought. I called on "Joe" and asked him what he thought.

At this point, my mom was clearly frustrated that I was not calling on her. The next thing I knew, she said, as clear as a bell, "This guy is really boring, isn't he?" I couldn't believe it!

To make matters worse, she leaned over to the lady next to her and said, "This guy is bad, let's get out of here!"

The next week at Mass, I asked the congregation how their week was. I told them I had a terrible week. It was so bad that even my mother took a shot at me.

† Monsignor John J. Enzler
Archdiocese of Washington, D.C.

OUR ARCHBISHOP, Robert Sanchez, was visiting the parochial school and preparing to offer Mass for the students. Before Mass began, he explained the various items that pertained to his office as bishop. He explained what the miter was and why he wore it.

Next, he came to the crozier. He asked the students, "Why do you think I carry this stick?"

Immediately, one of the kindergartners in the front row spoke up. "Because you're old!"

No one laughed harder than the Archbishop.

† Father James L. Vance
Archdiocese of Santa Fe

IN 1995, when I had been ordained only five years as a priest, I attended the installation ceremony of Archbishop John Clement Favalora of the Archdiocese of Miami. Since he was my ordaining bishop when he was in the Archdiocese of Saint

Petersburg, I felt especially privileged to be attending this most important event.

As I was getting on the elevator going down, I met a bishop who was getting on the elevator with me, but who wanted to go up. He was a tall man and I knew he was a bishop because he was wearing his pectoral cross. As he got on the elevator, he asked me if the elevator was going up. I told him no, it was going down. He then said, "That's okay, I'll ride along with you," which I felt was kind of him.

As soon as he pressed the button for his floor the elevator suddenly decided it was going up. I kiddingly said to him, "It seems you have more power than I do!" As we laughed, I introduced myself as David DeJulio from the Diocese of Saint Petersburg.

He then extended his hand and told me he was Roger Mahoney from Los Angeles.

As soon as he said that, my face turned flush! I stammered out, "Ca-Ca-Ca-Cardinal Mahoney?"

He then gave a big laugh, waved goodbye, and got off at his floor, leaving a red-faced young priest to wonder why God would do such a thing to him.

† Father David T. DeJulio
Diocese of St. Petersburg

†

IN THE EARLY FALL OF 1990, I was in Rome attending the seminary. There were a few occasions that I was able to meet the Holy Father. The first time, I was with our newly arrived class. We were in a private audience with the pope. There were only twenty-five of my classmates and the faculty from the college in attendance.

After the pope gave us a talk, we went up to meet him and shake his hand. As he came around to each of us, the rector of the seminary introduced us and then the pope gave us a set of rosary beads as a gift. I mailed my rosary home to my parents.

Three years later, on December 18, 1993, I was ordained a deacon. Prior to the ordination, my classmates and I were told that we would be granted an audience with the Holy Father. This visit with the pope would be extra special because we were permitted to bring our parents. Most of the seminarians' parents were able to come to Rome for the ordination. Sadly, my dad was dying of cancer at that time and was unable to attend.

I was with my father for Thanksgiving of 1993, but his health was rapidly deteriorating. There was actually some question if I would make it back to Rome to be ordained, but I did go back. Of course, my parents couldn't be in attendance.

On the day that we had the audience with the Holy Father, we were instructed that after he gave his speech, each of us could go up with our parents and meet him. Since my parents were unable to attend, I asked two priest friends, Father Jack Brennan and Father Tim Whalen, to come with me.

Since my last name begins with a "C," I happened to be the first one in the class to approach the pope. As the three of us walked up to the pope, he was flanked by a friend of mine, Bishop Thomas Tobin, and the pope's secretary. When we got up to see him, the pope cracked a joke and said, "Oh, these aren't your parents." I said no they weren't, and I introduced him to my two priest friends.

I told the Holy Father, "My parents couldn't make it because my dad is at home dying of cancer. I don't even know if I'll make it back home to see him."

I then asked the pope if he would pray for me that I would be able to get home to see my father one last time. He said to me, "I'll certainly pray for your father. Is your mother still alive?" I told him she was, and he asked what her name was and if I had any brothers and sisters.

I explained to the Holy Father how gravely ill my father was. The pope had his hand on my upper arm and he said to me, "Michael, I promise I will pray for you that you will be able to get home and see your father one last time." It was a very touching moment. I was teary-eyed and the other two priests were teary-eyed as well. I thanked the Holy Father and stepped aside so the next group of people could come forward.

The next day, December 19, early in the morning, I flew home. As I got to the airport in New York, there were three messages for me to call home immediately! I called home and I couldn't reach anyone. I tried all my relatives, too, and they were gone. I knew something was up. By this time, I was so tired and so upset, I missed my plane back to Pittsburgh. I begged the ticket agents to get me on another flight, and they did. When I finally arrived in Pittsburgh my brothers were right there waiting for me. They said, "We have to move quickly, there's no time to even get your luggage. We don't know if Dad is still alive!"

We ran through the airport and sped to the hospital. When I got off the elevator I made a left turn and saw all my relatives standing in the hall. My mother was standing among my relatives. She said, "He's been waiting for you."

I walked into the room and my mom closed the door so my dad and I could be alone. He couldn't really talk much, but his eyes were open and he knew I was there. I told him that I was there and that everyone else was there too. My mom told me prior to going in the room that the nurse wanted me to tell him that it was okay to let go. She said he'd been waiting for me and fighting to hang on.

I did tell my father that it was okay to let go. I also told him that as an ordained deacon, I was able to give him a blessing. As I knelt there, giving him a blessing, I glanced down toward his hand and saw his fingers wrapped around the rosary beads that the Holy Father had given me over three years before. After I blessed him, he closed his eyes and went into a coma. My father hung on for a short time afterward and passed away peacefully the next day.

My father was never one to carry rosary beads around and I don't know if I ever saw him pray the rosary. But I took that as a sign. I knew at that moment and I knew in my soul that the Holy Father had prayed for me the day before and that his request had been granted.

† Father Michael A. Caridi
Diocese of Pittsburgh

"God spoke to me. He said, 'Prepare yourself.'
I wasn't praying or seeking anything, but . . .
I stopped and asked, 'For What?'"

John T. Judie

A<small>S</small> A YOUNG BLACK
growing up in southern
Louisiana in the 1950s,
becoming a Black pastor in
an all-White suburban Catholic
church was a foreign concept.
After all, the Judie family were
devout Methodists.

*FATHER JUDIE'S JOURNEY to
ordination was delayed twenty
years from when he first
entered the seminary in 1963 to when he reentered in 1983.
He was ordained for the Diocese of Louisville in 1987.
He is currently pastor of Mother of Good Counsel Church in
Louisville, Kentucky. After completing only one full term as*

pastor, his parish received the prestigious Catholic Parish of Excellence Award in the fall of 2000.

In addition to being a gifted musician, Father Judie has created a global ministry program to aid the people of East Africa. His efforts have not gone unnoticed. In July of 1999, officials in Rwanda opened a care center for the orphans and handicapped children of that region. The center was named "The Mother of Good Counsel Rehabilitation Home for Handicapped Children and Youngsters."

Profile

THE HISTORY OF MY FAMILY was deeply rooted in the Methodist and Baptist faiths. There are Methodist preachers on my mother's side of the family and Baptist preachers on my father's side. Both sides have a history of talented musicians who have dedicated themselves to the church. Our family was also very close to the pastor.

I grew up playing with his children on a regular basis. Considering the time I spent with our pastor in the church setting and our home setting, I was drawn to him as a role model. I was the type of child that always loved to be in church. This goes back as far as I can remember. After Sunday school, my sisters and brother would head back home, but I would stay with my grandmother and enjoy main service. I was very observant and took in everything: the preacher, the choir, the musician, and all the dynamics of it.

It was 1959 when my mother made the decision about looking into the Catholic church. Some of her dissatisfaction had to do with the politics in the Methodist church at the time, but there were other reasons as well. Her reasons prompted her to look elsewhere. Sending her kids to Catholic school also seemed very attractive. I maintain my mother was "Spirit-led" in terms of looking at the Catholic church. She finally made the decision for herself and her five children to become Catholic. I was eleven years old.

As a Black family in the south, the larger issue wasn't so much turning to Catholicism as it was leaving the Methodist church. The greater sense of controversy was in part due to the fact that we had such strong roots in our family history in the Protestant faith. We are first-generation Catholics in our family and that was a major statement.

> Even though we were very new to the Catholic faith, we didn't feel too much out of place.

When we came to the Catholic church in 1959, it was pre-Vatican II. We had to adjust to the Mass being in a foreign language and the priest having his back to us. It took a while, but we were able to let go of the minister facing us and actually became used to the Latin Mass. There wasn't a great deal of participation at those beginning Masses. Our family always enjoyed full conscious and active participation in the Methodist church. One comfort we came to appreciate was that our parish happened to be African-American. Even though we were very new to the Catholic faith, we didn't feel too much out of place. After a few years of being Catholic, the church now said, "We want you to have full active and conscious participation." So we decided that God had ordered Vatican II just for us! That was the beginning.

Just like we were raised to be church involved in the Methodist church, we automatically became church involved in the Catholic church. I was an altar server with my brothers. Around the age of eleven I started taking piano lessons. I never realized I had a musical talent until I started taking lessons. By the age of twelve, I played the organ in the Catholic church for the first time. That started my career as a church musician. The first time I ever touched an organ was in the middle of Mass.

When the pastor came out to deliver the benediction, the organist wasn't there. I just took it upon myself and went up to the organ and started playing. It looked like a piano to me, so I just taught myself how to play the organ.

I always admired the pastor in my church, and I was very observant. We were always right in the middle of it. When I was in the eighth grade, I was visited by the vocation director for the Divine Word Fathers, who later became the first African-American bishop of New Orleans. I can remember him coming to talk with me about the priesthood and going into the minor seminary. I was very much ready and open to go for it even at that age. I wanted it. But my mother did not agree, partially because of my age, and partially because we had only been in the Catholic church for a couple of years. A lot of that was new and she never considered, at that point, giving up her oldest son to the seminary.

It was my very Methodist grandmother who opened up her eyes when someone said to her, "Don't you see that there is something special about this boy?" That's all she needed to hear. I entered the seminary as a sophomore in high school. It was 1963.

Phil Berrigan, the Josephite and member of the Catonsville Nine Group, taught me and mentored me as a high-school freshman long before he got into the eye of the media. He taught us religion, not theology. He taught us discipleship and ministry. We had a weekly report card of our spiritual life, daily prayers, how often we went to Mass, etc. We had to fill out this report card and hand it in every week. Along with our spiritual development and prayer life we were also required to bring in food for the poor. Something from our own kitchen to feed someone else. We had a food collection every week. I took it to the next step. On Friday evenings after school, I would go into the low-income housing where all the food was sent, and I would help them sort through it all. As a freshman in high school, I would walk through the low-income housing area carrying bags of groceries and just knocking on people's doors.

Although racism was in full swing in 1963, there weren't really any problems with me entering the seminary. The Josephite Fathers Community in Newburg, New York, was ministering to the Black Catholics in the South. They were attracting many students. The population at the time was about fifty-fifty Black versus White, so I felt very comfortable when I arrived.

> In December of 1966, I made the decision to leave the minor seminary.

In December of 1966, I made the decision to leave the minor seminary. I also said that I would never step into another seminary as long as I live. I was going through adolescence. I felt the people that were dealing with me didn't have a clue as to how to help me, or how to work with me. I always knew I could perform as a student, but in terms of personal development, it wasn't there. The seminary was still promoting and feeding us Irish spirituality. I didn't feel like I was in the right place, so I left.

After my seminary experience, I stayed in the North and migrated to Massachusetts. I stayed with some friends and began working at a state school for mentally retarded kids. In May of 1968 I enlisted in the Navy. My specialized training was in neurology and psychology. It was also very important to me that no matter where I was in my life, I was someone's church musician.

Prior to entering the Navy I was introduced to a priest who was friends with the same group of people I knew in Massachusetts. Coincidentally, he was entering the Navy around the same time. As fate would have it, we continued to see each other. We were assigned to the same bases in Philadelphia, California, and Japan. At each location, I was the musician and he was the chaplain.

91

During our last year in the Navy we were in Okinawa, Japan. For the months that we were together, Mike and I took that military chapel and turned it into a parish community. We worked hand in hand. We would go out in the community and socialize with the folks and have food and drink. We would also evangelize them and get them into church. In a matter of two months, he turned the Mass attendance from forty people to two hundred and thirty. These were all military folks. For Christmas-time we had a Midnight Mass. On Christmas Day, we had a Children's Mass. We tried to do it all "Parish Style." We also used an abandoned radar station for retreat weekends. Mike eventually left the priesthood. In many regards I felt he passed his ministry on to me. But I still did not realize I had a vocation.

When I left the Navy I had many job offers and opportunities. After various jobs and music ministries I ended up accepting a position in 1976 as choir director for a small non-denominational church.

Three years later, my father notified me that he was going back to Texas to live. All of my father's side of the family are very church involved. He has a brother who is a Baptist preacher and I also have a cousin who is a Baptist preacher. For my father to send me a piece of mail, the world had to had shifted. That's how earth-shattering this was. He was notifying me that he attended the installation of my cousin as pastor of a Baptist church in our home-town. The last time I actually saw this cousin was when we were both six years old. After all these years, I had no idea that we were developing and growing on parallel tracks. We were both involved in ministry

> I heard
> God say
> very clearly,
> "Prepare yourself!"
> I stopped
> and asked,
> "For what?"

and in music. That opened the door for me to reconnect with my cousin and uncle, who also is a Baptist minister. I was able to preach in both their churches. Around the time that this happened, God spoke to me. He said, "Prepare yourself!" I wasn't praying or seeking anything, but I heard God say very clearly, "Prepare yourself!" I stopped and asked, "For what?" I didn't hear an answer, but I could not help wondering what he meant.

I felt God was calling me to a preaching ministry. That ministry went on for four years before the call to the priesthood. I was still a practicing Catholic at that time. In the Catholic church if you are not ordained, you do not preach. That's a basic rule. I had a conversation with God and I asked him, "Hey God, did you forget I was Catholic? You called me to preach, but I'm Catholic." I didn't worry about it too much because I didn't know what to do with it or where to go with it, but God continually opened up doors and churches of different denominations. I didn't ask for this, but I kept getting invitations to speak in various churches. I actually began to finance my own ministry. I was still a Catholic, but I was preaching in a Baptist church. I would leave New York, fly to Texas, and rent a car just to have the opportunity to preach to thirty people. The trip would cost me five to six hundred dollars and I would only receive a twenty-five-dollar stipend.

In July of 1982, I was in Houston, Texas, preaching at my cousin's church. After the service I decided to pay a visit to a priest I had previously met. Fortunately, I was able to catch him at home. As we were sitting and talking, he was telling me about all the things he had been doing since taking over as pastor. I kept saying to myself, "I can do that." It was right then and right there when God spoke to me and said, "The priesthood is for you!" It was right there and it made sense. On the return trip to New York, the idea of the priesthood wasn't the struggle, it was more, "How do you do this?" I realized that if

God was truly calling me I wasn't going to worry about how, I knew it would get done. Some people don't catch the notion the way God works. First of all, God gives us what we need, then he calls us, as opposed to calling us first and then giving us what we need. But we must recognize it.

Since my call came in Texas, I decided to begin in Texas. I stayed in Texas for a short time, then I wound up in Chicago. While in Chicago, I received an invitation to do a gospel music workshop in an African-American parish in Kentucky. I came to Kentucky in July of 1983 to help with the workshop. I had never been in Kentucky before in my life. A priest friend of mine suggested I consider the Diocese of Louisville to become a priest. I told him I knew nothing about Kentucky, but I'd consider it. I wrote the bishop a short letter. When I went to Kentucky for the gospel workshop, I received a call from the vocation director. I met with him for four hours the day that I was to return to Chicago. I told the vocation director that I would return to Chicago and pray about it and if Louisville was still a consideration, I'd get back to him. After a short time, Louisville kept coming up. The only explanation I can give is that it "just felt right!"

I entered the seminary in August of 1983. I was thirty-five years old. I was in Saint Mary's in Baltimore. We picked that seminary because I was familiar with Baltimore. I accepted the seminary sight unseen. I was excited about getting started. But when I arrived, I wasn't sure if I was going to stay. I didn't even unpack! I lived out of a suitcase for three days. I couldn't tell you why I didn't like it, but I didn't. On the third day I decided to stay. While there, I was told I could go directly into graduate school. I studied for four years and received my bachelor's and master's degrees simultaneously.

My seminary experience was very different the second time around. Pre-Vatican II seminary was very oppressive. There was much more flexibility at Saint Mary's. I graduated from the seminary in 1987 and came back to Louisville. On August 1, 1987, I was ordained in the Diocese of Louisville. My mother and siblings were all able to make all of my ordination. I had to get used to my mother calling me Father Judie.

I didn't walk into the priesthood with any expectations. So there really is nothing that hasn't worked out, because I didn't expect anything. I feel, at least in my life, that there is a script that is already written. As I go from year to year or month to month, someone turns the page and I discover more of the script. There are so many things that have filled out my priesthood and ministry that I would not have asked for or not have dreamed of. For example, I am challenging this community to run a tuition-free school. Our parish has also put together a ten-year growth plan in spiritual formation for the community. For the next ten years the parish will actively work on its own spiritual formation.

Another aspect of my ministry is the East African Ministries. It is something I never would have dreamed of. It's a huge expanse that has put me in a global ministry position. In addition, I have established a Vocation Sunday. Once a year I bring in the vocation director to speak about vocations to the priesthood.

When someone is considering a vocation to the priesthood, I ask two questions: Why the priesthood and why you? An individual has to understand and recognize, is this a call from God, and what has God given them to empower them to answer the call? Once they understand that, then they know that this is what they need to hold on to no matter where they go. One of the questions I put to the

> When someone is considering a vocation to the priesthood, I ask two questions: Why the priesthood and why you?

seminarians is: "Are you a loving person?" Also, "Are you prepared to be loving to God's people?" I tell them I'm not interested in how well they can run a parish or how good they are at holding a big bank account. I don't care how well they can build buildings. Can they be, and are they prepared to be, loving to God's people?

Inevitably, the topic of celibacy is broached by anyone considering a vocation. I do not think the celibacy issue is a major concern. If it is, then they need to work it out before they go into the seminary because it will just be a distraction. Don't bring it into the formation process. Know that they are free enough to allow God to develop them and use them as God is calling them. They have to claim that sense of freedom. The problem is not celibacy, the problem is their trust in God! Don't you think that if God is calling you into the priesthood, God will enable you to be a celibate priest?

Celibacy, for me, guarantees me the freedom to be loving to everybody. I had to redefine for myself what celibacy means. I had to move it off the issue of getting married or not getting married. I've always understood that the ministry has to take precedence over everything else. That has always been inside me, long before I got the call to the priesthood. For me, when I look at my peers in the clergy who are married in the Protestant denominations, I also see a certain commitment to celibacy there. I remember a Methodist pastor once asked me, "So how do you do it?" "Do what?" I asked. He said the celibacy issue. I asked him how he did it. I asked him how he managed to be a good husband to his wife, a good father to his children, provide for his household, and take on the demands of running a church and congregation. I told him I knew one thing for sure, that if his wife was not as committed to the ministry as he was, he was living in a divided household. As a Catholic priest, I do not have that problem. The pastor agreed!

Yes, men have left the priesthood to get married. But I am not convinced that getting married is the main reason men leave the priesthood. I think they should be honest enough and have the guts to stand up before the congregation and tell them the main reason they want to leave. The issue of getting married is such a cop-out as far as I'm concerned. I told one parish, if you ever hear I'm leaving the priesthood, it's not because I want to get married and have children, it's because I'm sick and tired of putting up with your garbage!

It was interesting when I first came to my present parish. It wasn't the fact that I just looked Black, it was that I acted Black. That needs to be said. I preach very openly and freely and loudly as I would anywhere else. A good analogy is that I have more of a "Southern Baptist minister" style of preaching. Many times after I have preached the homily people will approach me and say, "Father, for a minute there I thought I was in a Baptist church." That's exactly what I sound like because that is where I developed and trained. That's what God gave me when he called me.

The present parish knew they were getting a Black pastor prior to my arrival. There was nervousness about receiving me. In this part of Kentucky, I was the first Black pastor ever, in White affluent suburbia, around Louisville. There is one other Black priest in the entire diocese.

The Wednesday before my first Sunday, I met with the worship committee. Some of them were very excited until I said, "I have heard all of the negative comments about my coming here already." Silence filled the room. I told them we could talk about it. I suggested that we put it on the table. Some on the committee were being told, "If he preaches for half an hour, I'm out of here. If he asks for an 'Amen,' I'm out of here. If he walks off the altar and plays the piano at Mass, I'm out of here." I told them not to do anything because there was nothing they could do. I also told them to not waste their time trying to explain or defend what I do. I told those gathered that I would address all their concerns on Sunday at my first Mass.

> "Who do the crowds say that I am?"

That Sunday, I got up to the pulpit for my inaugural sermon to read the Gospel, and would you believe that the reading in the Lectionary was Jesus asking the question, "Who do the crowds say that I am?" During that sermon, the body language of the congregation was screaming at me.

I am grateful, as unpleasant as it was, to have had the experience of growing up in the South, as a Black person in a segregated society. It enabled me to be able to recognize racial tension. I can see it and I know where it's coming from. I am better prepared to respond to it in a positive and productive way. I'm not in denial about it and I'm not going to let them be in denial about it.

Southern Louisiana, for most of its history, had the highest concentration of Black Catholics in the country. It's still the highest concentration today, but some of the dioceses have split. Our pastor at the time was White. These are some of the dynamics of the racism and segregation of the church as well as the state. The religious order priests were like missionaries to the Black churches and Native American churches. Although we have a concept of local church, and the bishop and the priest of our diocese were ordained for the whole diocese, they had nothing to do with these Black folk! They didn't consider them part of their responsibility. It was left up to the missionaries. As a result, when it came to Black vocations, most of them went into religious communities and not that many went into diocesan work. Many of them were not welcome as diocesan priests. One of the reasons was if an area didn't have any Black parishes, what were you going to do with this Black priest if you ordained him, send him to a White parish? Not in the segregated South you didn't.

It was comfortable for our family to be in the Black Catholic church. However, the missionaries who came from the religious communities were mostly from the North. Unfortunately, what was predominate was the fact that they ran the Black parishes but they taught "Irish spirituality." There was no concept at that time of recognizing or encouraging African-American spirituality. Anything that reflected the cultural context of the people, they imposed Irish spirituality or German spirituality.

The spirituality of an African-American Catholic church today is freer than that of a White Catholic church. Their spirituality is more freely expressed and shared. There is a very clear sense of spontaneity and worship. There is a very clear sense of the importance of interaction and an active worship on the community as a whole. There is a very clear sense of a different kind of interaction between presider, preacher, and the community. There is a dynamic in terms of preaching and praying. For example, there's a difference between the priest saying the prayer before the congregation where everyone is silent and a priest saying the prayers where people are constantly affirming every phrase through the prayer while he's saying it. You will hear the whole congregation praying out loud together. That is the difference between a sermon that is delivered where everyone sits quietly.

In an African-American church, that type of interaction is not orchestrated. There's not that sense of intimidation in a Black church that I've seen in White churches. For whatever reason, there seems to be a sense of intimidation and worrying about whether I said something out loud or spontaneously, what other people are going to think or if they're going to look at me oddly. Black folk just don't do that. There are a lot of Catholics who have been raised on Irish spirituality and they would be very uncomfortable with more spontaneous cultural expression. They have never been given that freedom or sense of affirmation. They are comfortable with the quiet Latin Mass, and that's okay, too.

It is most important for me, at least in my ministry, to be present for people and listen. I spend more time listening than I do anything else. I spend a great deal of time every week in counseling sessions, whether in the office, face to face, or on the telephone late at night. More than anything else, it's being able to give someone my total sense of attention and giving them that sense of freedom of comfort to open up. Then let God step in and do what God needs to do. I have had counseling sessions that have lasted over five hours.

> It is
> most important
> for me, at least in
> my ministry,
> to be present
> for people
> and listen.

In the role of pastor, I feel that God has given me a sense of vision in my leadership capacity. I'm not into maintenance ministry and I'm not a baby-sitter. I'm not here to just hold things together. I'm here to move things forward! God has given me a vision to help me move my community forward, to help the community grow more deeply in their own spiritual faith.

Part of my vision, what I hope to accomplish before I leave this church and this world, is for the parish to become spiritually healthy as a faith community. To pull them out of all of the baggage of the past and get it behind them. To provide a sense of long-term stability, but a sense of long-term self-assurance that they are doing what they are supposed to be doing. And finally, I would like congregations to shift the power and focus of their present and future life, not on the pastor who comes and goes, but on the community. The power and life of ministry rests in people who worship, not in the pastor.

"Father, why do you do that?"

In the Name
of the Father, . . .

IS IT BLASPHEMOUS for humor to be present in such reverent settings as a baptism or receiving the Holy Eucharist? When was the last time you went to confession?

AS CATHOLICS, there is no greater honor than to receive the sacrament of the Holy Eucharist. The Eucharist is the very heart of the Mass. Through the mystery of God, the priest trans- forms and consecrates ordinary bread and wine into the actual Body and Blood of Jesus Christ.

Similarly, when a child is baptized, he or she is cleansed from sin through the pouring of the water and the invocation of the Holy Spirit. The child is now a child of God and an heir of heaven.

During the celebration of a baptism or Mass, there is a certain decorum that is kept to maintain the sanctity, holiness, and grace of the ceremony. Decorum notwithstanding, unforeseen incidents occasionally occur that transcend all etiquette. And, despite the solemnity and sacredness of the confessional, the same is true for the sacrament of Reconciliation.

After many conversations with my pastor, Father Michael, I had decided to delete confession stories from my initial questionnaire. However, it just happened that the very first letter and story I received from a priest was about first confessions. As the weeks and months wore on I continued to receive confession stories that are inspirational as well as humorous.

What follows is an assortment of experiences that have happened to various priests, altar servers, children, and parishioners. Not only do the priests share their own humorous follies, but the occasional spontaneous remarks from children or members of the congregation that have brought laughter and fond memories of their priestly service.

I WAS IN FRANCE when I performed my first baptism, just before Vatican II. The French priests were really into including the people through ritual commentary, which is standard practice now, but it was new to me.

I was enthusiastically explaining all the gestures as I performed them: the anointing with the oil and charism, the white garment, the lit candle. I found myself quite impressive.

After the baptism, I went back to the sacristy with the father of the baby to fill in the baptismal register and I asked him, "What did you think of the baptism? Did you like the explanations?"

He said, "Well, yes, they were good, but . . ." He then paused, and got a perplexed expression on his face. "Didn't they used to pour water?" I had forgotten that gesture entirely.

† Father David B. Knight
Diocese of Memphis

ONLY A FEW HOURS after my ordination, I heard my first confession. We newly ordained priests had given our first priestly blessing to all present at the end of the Ordination Mass. Hours later, I was headed home with my family to prepare for my first Mass the next day.

Shortly after we arrived, Dad followed me into my old room and asked if he could have the privilege of being the first to receive the sacrament of Reconciliation from me. I was startled and dumbfounded. To think that Dad wanted to confess his sins to me! I've always had the greatest respect for my father's integrity and honesty. I knew how proud both Mom and Dad were of me on that ordination day, but I still felt very much like a boy when I stood beside them and compared my faith to theirs.

I don't know who was more nervous as I closed the door and sat in a chair while Dad knelt next to me. In the time Dad confessed his sins, I became even more aware of his goodness, his holiness, his love for the Lord. I shall never forget the incredible beauty of that time.

Psychologist Abraham Maslow describes such moments as "peak experiences," times when two people reach a new plateau in their relationship. This certainly was the case in my relationship with Dad at his confession. We both had tears in our eyes as I raised my hand and gave absolution.

Over the years, I've been privileged to administer the sacrament of Reconciliation to my mother and sister, countless friends, acquaintances, parishioners, and strangers. People come to be absolved from their sinfulness, their weaknesses, their ugliness. Sometimes after, they have wondered whether they would have the strength to admit to another human being what they have just shared. It fills me with admiration for their courage, their faith, and their love of Jesus.

I am amazed that I seldom remember the sins people confess. What I do remember is their trust and longing to be at peace again with God. Hearing confessions makes me aware of their struggles, their difficulties, and the crosses they have to bear.

I've wondered why I so often become aware of people's goodness when they confess. Then one day, after reflecting on this question, I gleaned insight. Each of us, of course, is created in the image and likeness of God. From my experience in the confessional, I've come to realize that, when we are honest with another person, the "image of God" in which we are made shines through. And when confronted with the image of God's goodness, love is our only possible response.

As a priest, the most beautiful times of the year for me are those weeks before Christmas and Easter when so many receive forgiveness. The long hours I spend administering the sacrament are not a chore, but rather a time in which I come to know and love my people dearly. My only regret is that so many others fail to understand and appreciate the beautiful gift Jesus has given the church in the forgiveness of sins.

Often, when I sit in the reconciliation room, I think back to that first confession with my father. I thank God for giving me that faith-filled man and those moments of grace.

† Father Joseph A. Miksch
Archdiocese of Omaha

THERE ARE TIMES while celebrating Mass, when the kids or altar servers do something funny, that I can barely keep myself under control from laughing. I actually pray fervently: "Lord, please help me get this laughter under control. No one will understand."

† Father Francis X. Meehan
Archdiocese of Philadelphia

IN MY FOURTEEN YEARS of priestly ministry I have had many joys, but none can begin to compare with the joy I feel when I share the Lord's forgiveness and peace with a penitent who has not known that peace for a long time. The most exciting and thrilling moments of my life have been within the context of the sacrament of Penance.

When I share this fact with others, especially with high school students, they sometimes look at me in disbelief. One student once commented: "Gee, Father, you must lead a very dull life."

I was grateful for the comment for it enabled me to share some of the more exciting moments of my life. One of my hobbies is that of snow and rock climbing. It is indeed a thrill to be standing on a ledge only two inches wide, four thousand feet up a vertical rock wall, while clinging to handholds half an inch wide and wondering how one will ever get out of that predicament. There's nothing quite like it for excitement. Yet after such climbs, I could fall asleep at night without too much difficulty.

I also happen to be a pilot and I love to fly. I've made several emergency landings and once did crash-land a plane. Talk about excitement! There isn't much more one can do for an encore. But after these experiences I was able to fall asleep at night within a reasonable length of time.

But what a thrill it is to share with penitents the peace of Jesus, to reassure them that it's okay. That he still loves them and in fact always has. After such wonderful and beautiful experiences my joy is so intense that sleep is often impossible. I can appreciate the truth of the words of Jesus when he says:

"I tell you, there will likewise be more joy in heaven over one repentant sinner than over ninety-nine righteous people who have no need to repent" (Luke 15:7).

† Father Joseph A. Miksch
Archdiocese of Omaha

105

ONE PARTICULARLY HOT SATURDAY, I had scheduled a baptism for a military family who was unable to have their baby baptized at the regular time, on Sundays. Not being used to Saturday baptisms, I went to spend some time visiting a sick friend. We were having a great old time when I suddenly realized that I was due back at the church.

I rushed back, arriving about forty-five minutes late. There they were, waiting and not the least bit annoyed. Or at least so they appeared. As I hastily prepared for the baptism, I inadvertently hit the large wooden board that holds the Hymn numbers. It was located precariously on a ledge about four feet above my head.

I glanced up. Too late! It was on its way down. It hit me on the forehead above my right eye. I realized that I was bleeding. I retreated to the sacristy and began to mop my bleeding head with paper towels. This took a while, as heads bleed profusely. I stuck my head out of the sacristy door and said, "I'll be with you in just a few minutes."

One of the godparents then asked, "Father, is this what they mean by baptism of blood?"

† Father Francis A. Diffley, M.M.
Diocese of Honolulu

AS A NEWLY ORDAINED PRIEST of five years, I was assigned as associate pastor to Saint Simon's in Ludington, Michigan. One sunny summer morning, I was the celebrant for the principal liturgy with full choir and church.

Prayer and worship were always a joy. At the presentation of the gifts, no one had filled the cruet with the sacramental wine for the Eucharist. I turned to one of the altar servers and asked him to go to the food pantry in the attached rectory and bring me a bottle of wine.

I waited for him to return, but he seemed to be taking his time. I decided to continue with the Prayer Over the Gifts and the Preface, certain that he would come back with the wine before I got to the Consecration. I soon reached the Words of Institution and Consecration, and still the little server did not return. The congregation was waiting with me in prayerful and reverent silence.

Finally, out of the corner of my eye, I saw the server return. I proceeded to the Consecration of the Bread, thinking I would pour the wine into the chalice without anyone noticing it. As I picked up the bottle the server had placed on the edge of the altar, I knew I was in trouble, as the bottle was square.

He had brought back, and placed on the altar, a bottle of Jim Beam from the pastor's private stock! Everyone laughed and chuckled. A choir member rushed to my aid, took the bottle of Jim Beam, hid it under his sport coat, and ran to the food pantry for the appropriate canonical Eucharistic wine.

At the end of the Mass, I mentioned that pure innocence was not knowing the difference between a bottle of altar wine and a bottle of Jim Beam. The following week, the story spread like wildfire. Everyone was saying that, in an attempt to gain more members, Saint Simon's was serving Jim Beam on Sundays!

† Father Paul Milanowski
Diocese of Grand Rapids

✝

I TREASURE those times when I have been privileged to witness miracles, evidence of God's grace at work in the lives of others.

One such incident happened on an Easter Sunday. It had been an extremely busy Holy Week, and I was celebrating the last of our Easter Sunday liturgies, looking forward to taking off for a visit with my family. Just as I set the lectionary down after proclaiming the Gospel and prepared to begin my homily, a man entered and stood in the back of the church. I could tell immediately that this was not the usual churchgoer. He was dressed in dirty blue jeans and a sweatshirt with the sleeves torn off; his hair was tangled.

It was terribly distracting to see him standing there and I really had to concentrate so I could get through my homily. Already I knew what to expect after Mass: he would camp on my doorstep, give me a long sob story, and ask for a handout. Just what I didn't need on this particular Easter Sunday.

Sure enough, after Mass, there he stood in front of the rectory. "Father," he asked, "can I talk to you for a few minutes?"

I tried to be polite as I invited him inside, but my thoughts weren't so kind: "Guess you know we'll give you a handout just to get rid of you."

He looked at me for a moment, then began to stammer. "I really don't understand why I'm here," he said. "When I left Omaha this morning for (he mentioned the name of some small town in South Dakota, which I no longer remember), I didn't even realize it was Easter. But somewhere along the way I took a wrong turn and ended up here.

"You know it's so strange," he said. "As I was approaching the outskirts of town, I became so curious. I decided to drive up and down the streets just to see what this town was like. And when I drove past your church and saw all those cars parked outside, I just felt such a strong urge to go inside to see what was going on. I walked in right as you were beginning your homily."

"I know," I thought! "You created such a distraction I forgot half of what I wanted to say."

But the stranger kept on with his story, and I remained silent. "I haven't been to church for ten or fifteen years," he said. "As I listened, you said something that really touched me. I wonder, would it be possible for me to get back in the church? Could I go to confession?"

I was not convinced he was sincere; I thought it might be part of a clever pitch for a handout. I questioned him about a few things, to see if there were any reasons why he couldn't receive the sacraments. There were none, so I helped him make an examination of conscience, after which he made a thorough confession.

Then I invited him back into church to receive the Eucharist. And I shared with him Luke's account of the appearance of Jesus to the disciples on the road to Emmaus; I related it to his experience of the Risen Lord on his way to South Dakota.

Afterward, as the man was getting into his car, he paused suddenly. "Father," he said, "I apologize for taking so much of your time. Please accept this as a token of my appreciation." He pulled out a twenty-dollar bill from his wallet.

As I drove home that afternoon, I kept thinking of his visit and tried to figure out what I'd said in my homily that so touched him. The more I thought about it, the more I came to believe that it was nothing I'd said or done. I simply had been given the privilege of being the lucky individual to witness a miracle of God's grace.

† Father Joseph A. Miksch
Archdiocese of Omaha

———— † ————

AN EVENT took place in December of 1999 that was, for me, one of the most profound experiences of my twenty-nine years of priesthood.

It's been my privilege to offer Mass at Saint Patrick's Cathedral in New York City during the past four years. December 8 was the feast of the Immaculate Conception. The cathedral was full. Christmas shoppers, office workers, and international travelers crowded into the pews or patiently stood along the side aisles.

The lector, music cantor, and I had entered the sanctuary and were starting Mass when I noticed a couple in their sixties move from the aisle into a pew where a younger fellow made some room for them to sit. They captured my attention immediately because the older fellow beamed a broad grin and nodded cordially.

He saw me watching him and his wife settle in and eyed me apologetically, but I smiled sympathetically. It was one of those little moments when two people have a spontaneous, brief exchange of good will and warmth. The liturgy was proceeding when, just before the Gospel, a muted chorus of voices drew my attention back to where my new acquaintance had been sitting.

Several faces turned to me in alarm and whispered all at once: "A doctor! A man here needs a doctor! A doctor . . . now!"

At the pulpit, I leaned into the microphone and alerted the congregation: "A man is in distress. If there is a doctor here, please come forward." Several men and a woman moved toward him.

Sensing things would soon be under control, we continued the liturgy with a sung prayer leading into the Gospel. But I had spoken only a few lines when an usher came toward me, stood by my side, and softly said into my ear: "He's dead, Father. His wife is asking you to come to him and anoint him. Now."

There she was in the midst of continuing efforts to revive her husband, summoning me to come. As I looked out to the congregation I was struck by the three thousand worshipers suspended in utter stillness and apprehension. If I had closed my eyes, I would have thought the cathedral was empty.

"I am going to tend to our friend here," I said. And in seconds, I had moved through the opening at the Communion rail and knelt next to the motionless man, who only moments before had been smiling at me.

A fellow priest arrived with sacred oils for anointing, so I stood to embrace his wife. She calmly explained that she and her husband were in New York celebrating their wedding anniversary. They had just come from the Radio City Christmas show and wanted to get to Saint Patrick's for Mass because it was there they had been married forty-three years ago to the day.

And then she said, "Bless you, Father, and all these people who are trying to help. Bless you. My husband couldn't be in a better place."

Returning to the pulpit in the silent presence of all in the great cathedral, my eyes searched the page for a place to resume the Gospel: "And Mary said: 'Behold, I am the handmaid of the Lord. May it be done to me according to your word."

No sermon was spoken. But I know Mary's words of whole-hearted acceptance of God's will had a profound meaning for us. Death and life, faith and hope, all come from God's loving hands.

† Monsignor Thomas McSweeney
Archdiocese of New York

ONCE, WHEN I was an associate pastor, I was in charge of the Easter fire at our Easter Vigil. Wanting it to be rather substantial, I had quite a bit of wood piled in a bricked-up pit that was burning beautifully.

The candidates for baptism were asked to gather around for the blessing of the fire. Arlis, one of the candidates for baptism, got a bit too close and when the flame leaped toward her, a spark landed on her leg. The spark instantly melted a hole in her nylon stocking. Arlis says to this day there is still a mark on her leg marking the time she was baptized a Christian!

† Father Richard J. Reiser
Archdiocese of Omaha

MY CAT, SEBASTIAN, remains a standard fixture in our parish life and attends Mass frequently. One Easter, he presided from the presider's chair at our two-hour Easter Vigil Mass on Holy Saturday night.

Sebastian has the character of a mighty lion, but the soul of a gentle angel. He has retrieved many a belfry bat from our twin bell

111

towers and dutifully laid them at my feet, or at the feet of my secretary, Joyce. Joyce, however, is always less than delighted by these tokens of affection, especially the "live" ones!

† Father Charles O. Mason
Diocese of Grand Rapids

IN OUR PARISH, we had a pastor who was very dignified. As is the custom before he presided, the pastor would bow before Christ and the Tabernacle. One day an altar boy was watching this and asked the pastor, "Father, why do you do that?"

The pastor replied, "I'm praying to God and I asked him to help me with my sermon."

The altar boy retorted, "Then why doesn't he help you?"

† Father Edward S. Jaksina
Archdiocese of Hartford

OUR CHURCH has ended up becoming a place where the "Gen-X" young adults come to worship. They gather in church with earrings all over their bodies. They wear spiked hair and different-colored hair. During Christmas of 1999, at Midnight Mass, I had a young man come to me during Communion. As he was receiving Communion, he took his hand and put it on my cheek. Almost like a love tap. I took it as an affirmation. It was such a tender move.

After that same Mass, a young man approached me whom I had never seen before and said, "Great homily." It made me feel very good.

Throughout Mass, I try so desperately to make our faith relevant. I enjoy talking about how God cares about our lives and what's going on in them. I try to encourage the congregation to just open up their life to God.

† Father C. Louis Martin
Archdiocese of Baltimore

"One of the reasons for my success is that I'm just an ordinary guy, and people know it!"

Joseph A. Miksch

H**e** IS SIXTY YEARS OLD. An avid rock climber and hiker. A licensed pilot for thirty-three years. A flight instructor. A man who has been on a honeymoon. A teacher who has touched the hearts of high-school students with his dynamic inspiration. A writer with such a command of the English language that his writing style seems more like a gift from the divine to inspire the faithful, rather  than just an occasional hobby. And, in his words, "just an ordinary guy." If that's not enough, Joe Miksch is a priest, too.

BORN ON NOVEMBER 25, 1940, Father Joseph A. Miksch shares with us his deep faith which was ingrained by the two most important people in his life, his parents. His outlook on life and his reflective insights into the priesthood give us a very real sense of his journey to the Kingdom of God.

Profile I THINK my vocation was implanted in me very early in life through my parents. They were very Catholic and very devout people. I grew up realizing that faith and religion in life are important. I always considered my mother and dad the ones who did the most for me in my faith. I often told them in my life that I've felt very small when I've compared myself to them as people of faith. I just wanted to do something worthwhile in my life that would truly help people and have lasting value. The priesthood seemed to be the natural thing for me.

I went through Catholic school all the way. In my day, we went to the minor seminary right out of grade school. We entered then partly because we didn't have a great public school system in our area.

When I talk about the seminary, I tell people that it was very similar to the Lincoln Penitentiary. The only difference was we had crosses on our turrets and they had machine guns. The seminary was not the greatest experience, at least as far as I was concerned. It was too strict for me because I'm a free-spirited kind of guy. One year I got to know the rector well because every other week I was being called to his office to be disciplined for playing pranks. There was the possibility of being dismissed. I guess I had a weird sense of humor. But it was a good education. I think of what college kids take today, usually twelve to fourteen credit hours. We took between twenty and twenty-four credit hours a semester. All we did was study. It was strict. But today it's much different for the seminarians.

In the seminary we were all told about the sacrifices we were going to have to make as priests. I'd like to get back to some of those priests and say, "Hey, who makes the sacrifices?" It's not us. I get a paycheck and I can spend it any way I want. I get a vacation and I take it whenever and wherever I want.

I've talked to many a husband who doesn't see his paycheck. He writes twelve bills and he may get an allowance for himself. He has a lot of responsibilities. In many ways, I'm freer than a lot of people. I can be independent, I can decide what I want to do and where I want to go. I'm very free in that sense.

> We didn't learn too much about the administrative duties in the seminary. I would love to go back . . .

We didn't learn too much about the administrative duties in the seminary. I would love to go back to the seminary and, instead of having a full semester on the Trinity, have a few weeks on the Trinity and a few weeks of business courses and personnel management. The one course I'd really love to take: the day the professor comes in, yells and screams and calls you every name in the book, and you have to remain perfectly calm and reflective. Most priests will tell you they enjoy the sacramental ministry. Being the administrator and the personnel manager can be very frustrating. However, there are priests who enjoy that part of ministry.

After ordination, I was first assigned to Saint Rose in Omaha. I was there for three years. I had a pastor who spoke as if he knew Moses personally. It was a difficult assignment because he was very much old school and didn't want me to go out with people or anything like that. I was basically confined. But the one great thing he did for me was to encourage me to take up flying. I fly planes to this day and just love it. He was not a pilot himself, but he had an associate who was a pilot with whom he got along very well. He thought that whatever his associate did was a good idea.

My first day on the job, I remember being met at the door by my pastor and introducing myself and being called "Sonny

Boy." Here I was, thinking that I had finally "arrived," and that's how I was treated. I learned a lot of humility the first three years. I was treated very much like a little child. But I was familiar with working with elderly people and I could deal with it. It didn't hamper me. I busied myself doing other things like studying. Although I never wanted to teach in a high school, I ended up teaching for twenty-five years. I actually couldn't wait for the first school year to begin, thinking I would drive around town and look at all the kids going to school and know that I didn't have to go back. Two weeks before school began, I received a letter from the archbishop saying, "You will be teaching!" Not, would you like to or would you consider it, just, "You will be teaching." Fortunately, I discovered a talent that I never knew I had. I really enjoyed teaching high school.

In the days of my early priesthood, we had curfews. We had to be back at the rectory by 11:00 P.M. It wasn't too many years before when we weren't even allowed to have a car. If you did have a car, you had to have permission from the bishop.

I don't remember ever second-guessing my vocation because of the restrictiveness. There were times when I became disillusioned thinking I had all the answers. Vatican II had just happened and out of it came new ideas. People had been satisfied with the old church and sometimes I wondered, "What am I doing?"

I see a lot of changes in some ways from when I was first ordained, but the basics are the same. We had a lot more freedom for a number of years after the council. Freedom to experiment and so on. Young men coming out today seem to be much more rigid in their thinking. They go very much by the book. For example, if I were to give a blessing for a fiftieth wedding anniversary, I would write an appropriate blessing for the event. Today, the younger guys will have to go directly by the church's book of blessings.

Every day in the priesthood is different. I'm up at 6:00 A.M.

I pray for about an hour. I have breakfast and then I'm ready to go. Once Mass is over, anything can happen, and it usually does. I'm very busy, but what I like about it is the variety of things that happen. A phone call can be a whole new experience, possibly leading to a lifelong friend or to an exciting adventure. I deal with all sorts of situations in people's lives. One excursion took place after counseling a couple in pre-marriage classes. We became friends and I asked where they were planning on taking a honeymoon. I suggested the Grand Tetons in Wyoming. It's such a beautiful place. I told them that I'd happily fly them out there if they were interested. After a few weeks went by, the bride-to-be called and asked if I was serious. After marrying the couple on a Saturday, I flew all three of us off to their honeymoon. It was a magnificent week with breathtaking surroundings. Not many priests have been on honeymoons, so I like to boast about that. It's just another service I provide!

Dealing with the people can be most fulfilling. Preaching and several statements that people have made have really helped me pull it all together. One lady said to me, "It must be nice to have a job where you know you can touch people's lives and really make a difference." I am very much aware of the fact that I have an opportunity to do that. Another person said to me, "Priests are so lucky. You get to deal and work with the best of people." Ever since hearing that I realize how lucky I am because I really do deal with wonderful people. I mean parishioners, young and old alike. I am really inspired by young people who are starting families and who are deeply rooted in the faith. I enjoy being involved in the sacraments, reconciliation, counseling, and listening to people's problems. People confide in me and share things with me that they wouldn't share with anyone else. I consider that to be such a privilege.

I enjoy counseling a great deal. You're helping people when they need you the most. I did have difficulties with

> It was
> a significant
> turning point
> in my life
> when I discovered
> that priests
> don't have to be
> answer people.

counseling my first couple of years after ordination. I thought the priest had to be the answer man. I thought every other priest had that power, but I realized I didn't have all the answers. It was a significant turning point in my life when I discovered that priests don't have to be answer people. Finally, after a few years, I went back and learned how to be a counselor. Through my courses the first thing I learned is that counselors don't give advice or solve problems, they listen. That took a tremendous burden off my shoulders because I learned you didn't have to have the answers. You just need to listen and help people reflect on their own problems. Usually, they can solve their own problems. That was a tremendous insight for me. When I first started, I didn't have a lot of self-confidence. From the responses of people I've counseled, I came to realize that I do have talent and ability.

I really didn't have any goals when I left the seminary. I sometimes think I was pretty immature in that regard because a lot of priests I talk with have had all these goals and dreams. Maybe I didn't even know what I was getting into completely. I do know one thing, God is very present through me. During anointings, reconciliation, and counseling. Sometimes with preaching, you know that the Spirit is working through you. I think of the healing ministry in the Gospel as Jesus felt power going out of him. Once in a while you get that feeling. You can't really describe it but you know something is happening beyond you.

One of my hobbies is rock climbing. I enjoy telling the story about how after days and days of cloudy, dreary weather, I was assigned to one of the higher trails during a climb. We got above the clouds and the sun was shining and we were in the dry air and suddenly I had this experience of God's presence and the beauty of nature. I refer to that as a moment of transfiguration. I think everybody has those moments where maybe something happens and you experience the presence of God in a special way. I've talked to parents who have had no religion at all and yet they felt the presence of God or his power when they needed help. I like to talk about moments like that. I have those peak experiences or moments once in a while. From what I've read in John of the Cross, these things happen, but there's nothing you can do to make them happen; they're God's gifts. I hope everybody has these moments and experiences. It's just a matter of being aware of them.

I've really been very blessed in my ministry. There haven't been any expectations that haven't worked out. I recently went back to my first ordination class reunion after thirty-five years and I came away realizing how lucky I've been. There were twenty-four guys who were ordained that year. Twenty of us were at the reunion. And some have left the priesthood since being ordained.

When I hear about priests leaving the priesthood, I often wish we could be grateful to them for the years of service they gave rather than think of them as betraying the church. I realize that some people simply aren't cut out for the priesthood. At least in my day, the seminary training I had and the reality of the priesthood are very different. Some people got into the priesthood without realizing what it was really all about. Back in the 1960s sometimes there was a lot of pressure for parents who knew it would be a great thing to have their son be a priest. I know that some became a priest for the wrong reasons.

Today it's just the opposite. That pressure is not there. People don't encourage their sons to consider the priesthood, which is sad. The one thing I tell people is that, although we've been blessed in our area, I have job security. The Spirit is touching us all the time. Two of our present priests are kids I taught in high school. I would tell any man, young or not so young, to definitely consider the priesthood very strongly as an incredible opportunity to serve God's people and have a good life. Just simply to be open to the Spirit. I can only recommend it. I've done a lot of things in life but I've never found as much satisfaction as I do in the priesthood.

The Catholic church needs more priests. I know for some, celibacy is an issue. I believe if celibacy was an option, we'd gain a few in numbers, but I don't think it would be the sole issue. In jest, I've told the archbishop, "If you pay us what they pay baseball players, twenty thousand per Mass, you'd probably have more vocations." Although I can see advantages of being married, I can see problems, too. I deal with enough married couples having problems so I know it's not the answer. I certainly don't think lifting the ban on celibacy will solve our vocation situation, although I would like to see it as an option. Our Protestant friends, who are allowed to marry, have just as much a shortage of ministers as Catholics do. A good friend of mine who is a Lutheran minister expressed the same thoughts.

I once shared in a homily that if the church ever changed the law that priests could marry, I would probably marry, that is, if somebody would marry me. For me, I find the celibacy issue hardest to deal with when I'm transferred and have to start all over again. It's such a lonely feeling and I think of how wonderful it would be to share my thoughts with a spouse or a family. I know for some priests the loneliness is what completely gets to them. On the other hand, I just love being alone because of some of the things I do. It hasn't been as hard for me. When I get transferred, I go through a grieving process that takes me about a year. I become so close to people because they share so deeply with me. One week I know everybody and know all sorts of things that no one else knows.

I have relationships. The next week I know absolutely nobody and I have to start all over again. That's tough!

One thing I've learned over the years is we have to be patient. We hear the statistics, 40 or 50 percent of the people attend Mass. Very often the inactive people today will be the ones who are running the parish and doing everything five years from now, or ten years from now. It's when the Spirit touches them. We have to allow the Spirit to work in his time. I see this happening all the time; we have to be patient. What I want isn't really all that important and what I do isn't really that important. It's what the Spirit does in different situations. I am very hopeful because there are so many good things happening. The Spirit is very much alive!

Everybody has qualities that enable them to serve. There are many qualities that I bring to my ministry. I have a very deep faith and I think it's authentic. I would never preach on anything unless I really believe it. I come across in a nonthreatening way. In the seminary, I used to admire the guys who were very assertive, but I like the fact that I don't come across that way. I'm a good listener and in a sense I'm a very simple fellow. I believe I reach people at about a fourth grade level. They understand that. I try to take theology and bring it down to that level, too.

> I often think to myself how narrow my life would be if I weren't a priest.

One of the things I enjoy so much about my priesthood is the opportunity that so many doors are open to me. I can get to know so many people. Even though I preach to a couple thousand people over a weekend, it's impossible to know them all. But they get to know me. Instead of preaching at them, if I share with them just who I am in my faith and in my homilies, they do get to know me. I often think to myself how narrow my life would be if I weren't a priest. Whatever I'd be doing, I'd only meet a limited number of people. I'm sort of a shy guy by one sense so I wouldn't be outgoing, but priests are forced to be.

I tend to get frustrated with some priests I know who show no enthusiasm! They look at the ground all the time when they talk, or they just read their homilies. I grab my mike and go down the aisle and just chat. I try to show some enthusiasm and excitement. It's frustrating watching a priest who comes across as functionary. We need to just be ourselves. We need to be enthusiastic and it's got to show. Unless it does show we're not going to convince anybody about how wonderful it is to be a priest. It was a great philosopher who once said, "If Christians believe that Jesus rose from the dead, then they ought to start acting like it!" When we respond, the people will respond.

The biggest surprise to me in thirty-three years as a priest is the way God works through ordinary people. Sometimes it just blows me away. Friendships along the way have really helped me grow. Healing experiences have really touched me. All I would like to do is to be able to touch people's lives and help them come to know the Lord Jesus on a personal level.

People need to realize that priests are just as ordinary and human as everybody else. One of the reasons for my success is that I'm just an ordinary guy, and people know it! People need to see priests that way. We don't have all the answers, and we're not saints. We have our weaknesses, too. We get tired, crabby, and grouchy like anyone else. We enjoy things like anyone else. We're sinners, too, but we believe in the Lord Jesus and we're on a journey to his Kingdom.

I hope folks see me and other priests as being happy. I enjoy what I'm doing! I hope people would see me as being authentic, that I really believe what I preach. It is also my hope for people to see me as a man of faith, because that's what matters, and to realize that it is indeed a privilege to be a Catholic priest!

5

"Father, could you come quickly?"

We Are
Gathered . . .

$\mathbb{D}\textcircled{O}$ YOU REMEMBER planning your wedding as if it were opening night on Broadway? Did you ever consider that many priests may not enjoy doing weddings? Are you under the impression that presiding over a funeral is one of the more difficult tasks for a priest to perform? Are you aware of the amount of time a priest spends visiting the sick?

FINALLY, the day you've waited for your entire life has arrived. You've fantasized about it, planned for it, and prayed for its success. You've visualized what it's going to be like to walk down the aisle in your flowing white gown, as the love of your life is looking on. The family and friends you've invited are all talking about how beautiful you and your soon-to-be spouse look. It's your day and nothing can go wrong. Right? Don't count on it.

As I spoke with priests across the country, I was surprised to learn of the difficulties they can have with weddings. Priest after priest echoed the same sentiment, their frustration over the casualness people display toward the sacrament of marriage.

Yet I find it interesting that many of the priests expressed joy in presiding over funeral Masses. The pleasure of celebrating the person's life, and the spiritual comfort priests offer in a time of grief, can be very rewarding, not only for the grieving families, but for the priests as well.

Although hospital work and calling on the sick may not seem glorious to some, it remains a vital part of a priest's job. Notifying the parents of a young parishioner killed in a car accident or hearing the last confession of an elder church member just before he slips into eternity are some painful moments that come with the territory. The courage and compassion, the tenderness and empathy that priests exhibit during these defining moments are testimony to their faith.

And through it all, there is often a lighter side.

A SOON-TO-BE MARRIED young couple came to the rectory one evening for the usual preparation for marriage session. The bride was carrying a small dog in her arms, and it was apparent she intended to hold on to him for the entire session.

When I told her that I was allergic to dogs, and that she would have to leave the animal in an adjoining room, she was obviously disgruntled, but did comply.

Before they left that evening, the young lady requested permission to carry her dog down the aisle with her on her wedding day. The young man appeared to be very uncomfortable with her request.

My response to the groom was, "You don't have to show up tomorrow, Jim. She'll be marrying her dog."

† Father Joseph Parel
Archdiocese of Hartford

DURING MY THIRTY-ONE and a half years of ministry, I must have taken part in some two hundred weddings. Whenever I hear that the bride and groom intend to have very young children as wedding attendants, I almost always cringe. I remember episodes of terrified three- or four-year-old kids coming down an aisle bordered by standing adults with cameras ready to "shoot" the cute children parading in front of them. I would almost classify some of these episodes as child abuse.

On the other hand, "Dear Abby" has printed letters of brides who, wanting "the perfect wedding," would outlaw any children from attending their wedding. They give as the reason for excluding children from their wedding the unpredictability of children in a well-orchestrated affair. Some brides are afraid children will "steal the show" from them. This is to be their event.

Recently, I was taken aback when I was informed at a wedding rehearsal that not just one, but six children would be attendants, ages varying from five to ten! I bit my tongue, while saying to myself, "The bride will soon find out what a mistake this was!" To my surprise, the children all came down the aisle without any fuss and did quite well.

When it came time to rehearse the exchange of vows, I hesitated, since I usually recommend that the wedding attendants surround the bride and groom for that event. I looked at the bride and groom and asked if they would like to have the children around them during the exchange of vows. Both bride and groom exclaimed, "Could they?"

They did beautifully on the wedding day, even after staying up late the previous night because of their joyful presence at the rehearsal dinner. I must say their presence gave a special meaning to what was happening.

I soon discovered there was a special relationship between these children and their aunt and uncle. It was impressive to see the bride and groom dancing with the children at the reception. This couple was definitely a modern-day expression of the pied piper.

The words of Jesus, when the apostles were trying to keep the children away from him, also came to mind: " 'Let the little children come to me; do not stop them; for it is to such as these that the kingdom of God belongs. In truth I tell you, anyone who does not welcome the kingdom of God like a little child will never enter it.' Then he embraced them, laid his hands on them and gave them his blessing." (Mark 10:14–15)

As I look back, I see the specialness of that newly married couple. Their love was joyful, nonpretentious, gentle, and kind, reaching out to everyone there, old and young alike.

It was truly an image of Jesus' inclusive love in their relationship: a sacrament of God's love.

† Father Roger P. Chabot
Diocese of Portland, ME

IT WAS A SAD DAY. Old Mrs. "B" had died. Her grandson was band director at the local high school. He wanted to make sure everyone in attendance was able to hear the service. So he rigged up amps, microphones, and wires throughout the church for the funeral liturgy.

At the time, I was wearing a lapel mike.

About six blocks away, there was a lock and dam located on the river.

As Mrs. B was being wheeled into church, the lock-master's voice came over our PA system loud and clear and said, "Give the old girl a good kick and she will get through there!"

A loose mike jack—and a barge stuck in the lock!

† Father Edward R. Schleicher
Diocese of Pittsburgh

I USUALLY WRITE the names of the couple getting married on sticky pieces of paper all through the book that I use at the wedding. But one time I did not, saying to myself it would not be necessary because I knew this couple so well.

When it came time for the vows, I told the groom to repeat after me: I, George, take you to be my wife. At first he did not respond, so I repeated myself, thinking he was just too nervous. Again, he did not respond. In fact, he kind of looked at me with a blank stare, then finally said, "My name is not George!"

Everyone at the wedding just howled with laughter and I think I turned about every shade of red you could imagine. Eventually, we did get the couple married and to this day, I still call him George when I see him.

† Father Raymond Moss
Diocese of Cheyenne

MINISTERING in the heart of Appalachia is, of necessity, ecumenical in scope. This is especially true when it comes to funerals.

I recall one particularly memorable funeral of a man whose untimely death was the result of injuries sustained in a freak automobile accident. He and his wife had both been baptized in the Old Regular Baptist Church, one of the so-called "Primitive" or "Hard Shell" Baptist churches so plentiful in southern Appalachia.

Despite the often fierce anti-Catholicism of these Primitive Baptist churches, the widow of the deceased approached me, requesting that I celebrate a funeral service for her husband. The request was not too surprising, really. This particular couple had long ago fallen away from regular participation in the Old Regular Baptist Church, and, since their oldest child had been enrolled in our parochial grade school, their closest church affiliation was with our local Catholic parish.

I agreed to celebrate a scriptural wake service at the funeral home on the evening of the visitation, and funeral liturgy outside of Mass in the church on the following day.

The rather cold reception at the funeral home was not too surprising to me. Nor was I surprised that many of the deceased's family members, all of them devout members of the Old Regular Baptist Church, refused to come to the funeral liturgy at the church.

I had learned the evening before that many of them thought I was going to baptize the deceased at the funeral service. It didn't take much thought on the matter to realize that someone, somewhere along the line, had mistaken the Rite of Sprinkling, celebrated at the beginning of the funeral liturgy, for an actual baptism.

I did my best during the liturgy to explain the meaning of the various ritual actions: the clothing of the body with the funeral pall, the use of the Paschal candle, and, of course, the true meaning of the Rite of Sprinkling as merely a reminder of our baptism.

Some of the family may have been offended by the reading of the Sacred Scriptures by a woman; the Sister of Mercy who works as our school principal proclaimed the first two readings and the responsorial psalm.

Women are not permitted to do that in their tradition. Nor do they have a tradition of singing hymns, except in the tradition of "line singing" when led by recognized elders within the congregation. All things considered, the liturgy proceeded rather smoothly, and even a few compliments on the ceremony were offered by some.

Finally, when the liturgy had come to an end, we proceeded to the site of the interment: a single hand-dug grave halfway up the side of a steep mountain. It was a miserably bleak, gray, rainy day, and the ground was muddy. The pall-bearers labored to haul the casket up the steep hillside, trying, often unsuccessfully, to gain each foothold on crude steps dug into the earth with the same shovels used to dig the grave. Once the pallbearers reached the grave site, the casket was placed on two two-by-fours which straddled the open grave.

The grade was so steep that the pallbearers had to hold the handles tight on the casket in order to prevent it from slipping down the hill. The casket did begin to slide several times, but each time the frantic efforts of the pallbearers to regain their hold were successful.

After I had recited several prayers, I stepped aside to allow family members to say their final farewells. To my surprise, the casket was opened once again, and while the pallbearers continued their struggle to maintain their grip, family and friends were throwing themselves over the body. It was a display of mourning that would rival the most respectable of Italian wakes!

One of the more moving displays was that of a young man, dressed in work boots and overalls, who gathered the family dog in his arms and held him up in clear view of the casket.

As the family continued their ritual, I decided to move out of the way so that the family would have more room on the steep and heavily wooded site. I found my way quietly down the steep pathway to the road below and made my way among the cars and pickup trucks that lined the narrow dirt lane.

As I approached the vehicle in which I would be riding home, a stately looking woman approached, and I recognized her to be the grandmother of the deceased. She was, I would later learn, the wise matriarch of a very sizable clan indeed.

She thanked me for celebrating the funeral, and she apologized for those members of the family who had refused to participate and begged me to excuse them for their misunderstanding of my Catholic faith.

Although I had already excused those family members who had not participated, I deeply appreciated her kind words and her loving consideration of my own predicament.

The entire event left me with a sense of peace, knowing that the walls of ignorance that still stand between so many of us are not quite as insurmountable as they so often seem and I am led to pray even more fervently for the unity Christ so ardently desires among his disciples.

† Father Leonard A. Smith
Diocese of Wheeling-Charleston

ONE EVENT that stands out happened in December of 1999. At the conclusion of the funeral of a parishioner, prior to the final prayers and dismissal, one of the parish leaders stood up to give some remarks in the name of the Holy Name Society to which the deceased had belonged.

He spoke about the deceased, a seventy-seven-year-old man, who had so graciously and positively affected parish life in general. He noted how he had truly been a role model as a man, a Christian, a Catholic, and a husband and father.

He called on the members of the parish to not forget his wife and daughters after the funeral was over, reminding folks of how many people had spent so much time with the family during his illness in support and prayer. After it is over, people can so quickly forget, just when they are needed most.

When the Mass had ended, some of the members of the parish with whom I am very close came up to me. They said, "Father Rick, when Albert talked about keeping up with the family now, it dawned on my husband and me that when this is all over and finished, you are left all alone to deal with your sadness and grief, and that you have been doing that ever since you came here. We want you to know that we are here for you, too, and we want to do whatever we can to ease your grief as well."

It struck me that night, as never before, that most times, parishioners don't realize how difficult it is for parish priests to bury people they have grown close to over the years, and that we, too, need an opportunity to mourn, to grieve, and then to celebrate new life in the resurrection.

† Father Richard R. Andrus
Archdiocese of Saint Louis

THE TIMES that I am called out in the middle of the night have been the times where I have felt most like a priest. You're there, in life-and-death situations, and it just dawns on you that this is why you were ordained: to come to people in their hour of need. Never once did I leave a hospital room or emergency room where I wasn't grateful to the Lord and didn't thank the Lord on the way home for letting me get the call to go out.

† Father Michael A. Caridi
Diocese of Pittsburgh

✝

I SERVED as a chaplain at Mercy Hospital in Pittsburgh for many years. One Halloween weekend I was called to the emergency room to anoint a man who had been brought in with a heart attack. While I was waiting for his family to arrive, I began strolling through the halls of the hospital.

Coming from the opposite direction was a woman dressed as a cat (a la the musical "Cats"). She had been partying at a downtown night spot, had fallen and broken her arm, and now was sporting a freshly made cast on her left arm.

Close behind her was a man dressed as a pirate, with an eye patch and a fake parrot on his shoulder. Rounding the corner, I saw a nun standing near one of the examining rooms. Knowing that she had seen the cat and the pirate, I went up to her and said, "Are you a real nun, or are you someone dressed as a nun?" "Oh no," she quickly replied, "I'm a sister from the Sister's Motherhouse, and I've brought Sister Mary Immaculata into the hospital."

Without missing a beat, she added, "But are you a priest or someone dressed as a priest?"

✝ Father Charles W. Speicher, Ph.D.
Diocese of Pittsburgh

✝

I RECEIVED A CALL from a parishioner on a Saturday evening. It was about fifteen minutes before Mass. "Father Joe," he said, "we just took my wife to the hospital. She is suffering terrible chest pains. Would you come?"

Knowing I could not get back in time for Mass, I told the man that I would be there right after Mass. "Father," he said, "that may be too late."

Sensing the urgency in his voice, I rushed over to church and asked a parishioner to tell everyone I'd had an emergency call and would get back as soon as possible.

When I arrived at the hospital, the woman was in the special care unit. She was in such intense pain, in fact, they were giving her morphine. I gave her absolution and anointed her.

"Give life and health," I prayed, "to our sister on whom we lay our hands." Before I did so, I explained to the woman that Jesus often reaches out and touches people with healing power. I told her I would now place my hands on her head and ask Christ to touch her with healing power. As I placed my hands upon her head, I prayed with all the fervor of my heart.

The next day, I visited her again. A few days later, she was well enough to return home.

The following Sunday I took her Communion. After our visit, her husband accompanied me to the car. "Father Joe," he told me, "last week when you went to the hospital, my wife was in such pain she didn't think she could stand it anymore. But when you laid your hands on her head, the pain left her immediately."

We were silent for a few moments. "Perhaps," I said, "the morphine was beginning to take hold." "No," he said, shaking his head, "that wasn't it."

Now, I have no idea why the pain left that woman at the moment I laid my hands upon her head. It may well have been the morphine. Then again, I have seen recoveries take place after the laying on of hands and anointing of the sick.

I do believe that God sometimes does choose to exercise healing power through me. When that happens, I can only step back in fear, wonder, and awe, as I ask myself, "Is it really possible? WOW!"

Jesus truly does touch people through me. So often when I am privileged to witness miracles of grace and see the saving power of God at work among us, I can only step back and thank God for choosing me to be a priest. As I reflect back on my twenty-five years of ministry, I am especially grateful for those moments when I have been privileged to witness God's power at work among us, God's miracles of grace.

† Father Joseph A. Miksch
Archdiocese of Omaha

PRESIDING OVER A FUNERAL can be wonderful, especially if you knew the deceased, who they were, what made them tick, etc. It enables me to speak honestly about the person.

† Father C. Louis Martin
Archdiocese of Baltimore

IN OUR SCHOOL, we had a custom of attending the wake of any deceased relative of any of our students.

Once, the principal and I attended the wake of a student's deceased relative. When we arrived at the funeral home, we went to the casket to offer a private prayer. As we were praying, I told the principal that I thought we were at the wrong wake.

He whispered to me, "How do you know?"

I said, "Because the man in the coffin is wearing a Yamaka!"

† Father Michael Kolodziej, O.M.F.
Diocese of Springfield, MA

WHAT A SHOCK it was to many parishioners when I attended the reception of a wedding I had just witnessed, and danced nearly every dance. To make matters worse, I was very young, around thirty, and had just become pastor only months before.

By the time Sunday Mass began the following morning, word had spread through the neighborhood and parish of the "wild priest" who knew how to dance to the latest R&B music.

What an eye-opener that was to a church that never saw a priest on a dance floor!

† Father Richard R. Andrus, S.V.D.
Archdiocese of Saint Louis

THE FOLLOWING IS an account of my first day "on call" after arriving at my first assignment as a priest of the Archdiocese of Philadelphia. The parish was Saint Canisius in Mahanoy City, Pennsylvania. I arrived at this parish on Saturday, following the feast of the Ascension, in May of 1952.

On Monday, as we were preparing for the funeral of one of the parishioners, we received a call that the sister of the deceased had had a heart attack while bidding her brother farewell.

I was on call, as I said, so this was to be my first anointing and sick call. I rushed over to the house, where the wake had taken place, as was custom in those days.

While anointing the woman, she died with a last gasp. I then returned to the church for the funeral of the initial parishioner.

That afternoon, the collieries of Mahanoy City had a serious accident, and I was called to anoint the victims. Upon arriving at the colliery, I was given a hard hat, boots, and heavy coat, and then I descended into the mine with the miners. Upon reaching the level of the accident, we moved on to a tracked coal car and proceeded to the place of the accident. Two men

135

had been killed, two injured, and two escaped without injury. I anointed the two who had been killed. We returned to the surface and the mining authorities asked if I would inform the families of the deceased.

In this case, it was the wife of a Mahanoy City man and the parents of a Shenandoah Heights man. I did as they directed, bringing the sad news to the respective wife and parents.

That evening there was an emergency at one of the "patches," a settlement of mining families nearby the parish. We were having supper, the pastor and I, and the pastor indicated that he would accompany me on this emergency to assure that everything went well.

By this time, I was feeling like a veteran of emergencies, but he did go with me to anoint this member of our parish. These three incidents, and five last rites, made up my first day of active priesthood in 1952.

† Monsignor Robert T. McManus
Archdiocese of Philadelphia

ONE DAY I WAS CALLED to the hospital room of a patient who was dying of cancer. The doctor had informed the patient and his wife that the cancer had advanced to the stage where he had only a couple days left to live. I administered the sacrament of the Anointing of the Sick to the patient and gave him the Apostolic Blessing.

After leaving the patient's room, I told the wife that she could call me and that I would be willing to pray for him again. Two days later, the wife phoned me to ask whether I could come to the hospital room to pray for her husband. The end was very near. We agreed to meet in her husband's hospital room at one o'clock that afternoon for prayer.

When I arrived at his room, he was very weak and could only whisper a few words. After taking his hand and offering a prayer for strength and consolation as he prepares to meet his maker, the patient whispered something to me at the end of the prayer. I asked him to please repeat what he had said. Again, I couldn't understand the few words that he was saying to me. He repeated this three times.

Finally, I asked the wife if she would ask her husband what he was trying to tell us. She leaned over very close to his head and said, "Honey, please tell me what you are trying to say." He repeated his few words to her. She looked up at me and said, "He wants to know whether that is a hairpiece that you are wearing."

I assured him that I have all my natural hair and that I wasn't wearing a hairpiece. The patient smiled as he slipped into eternity after having been fortified by the sacrament of the Anointing of the Sick and with the knowledge that the priest who anointed him wasn't wearing a hairpiece.

† Father Hugo L. Blotsky, O.S.B.
Diocese of Bismarck

I ANOINTED A MAN who was terminally ill with cancer and asked him to offer up his sufferings for someone who needed that special grace of conversion. Less than twenty-four hours later a man appeared at my doorstep. He wanted to go to confession. He had been away for thirty-two years. After celebrating the sacrament with him, I asked him why he had chosen to come that particular day after staying away for so many years.

He looked at me, shook his head, and said, "Father, I really don't know. I'm not from this area. I was driving into town and saw your sign along the highway. I suddenly felt I needed to do something to straighten out my life with God. I really don't know how to explain it."

Less than an hour later another man came to my door. He had been away for more than twenty years and his story was almost the same.

I first thought these were just coincidences, but not anymore.

† Father Joseph A. Miksch
Archdiocese of Omaha

> "Each one of us can truly find the person we are
> when we respond to God's grace."

Donald Kane

Through MY
CHILDHOOD years, our family
moved to various states in order
for my father to advance in his
company. One of our stops was
a three-year stay in Louisville,
Kentucky. My brother, two sisters,
and I seemed to adapt to our new
surroundings quite well, and it
wasn't long before all of us fell into
a routine and quickly made friends
in our new neighborhood.

*ONE BENEFIT we had with this particular transfer was being
closer to a family member who lived not far from Louisville*

in a town called Trappist, Kentucky. As a lad of only seven years old, I didn't find anything unusual about our visits to Uncle Bill, also known as Brother Donald. As a matter of fact, I thought it was quite normal to see him in brown or white robes. My uncle was a Trappist monk at the Abbey of Gethsemani.

We lived in Louisville from 1968 to 1971. Although my memories of the monastery have somewhat faded, those that remain are cherished to this day. The visits with my Uncle Bill were great fun. Picnics with my family, including Uncle Bill and Brother Patrick Hart, were always something to look forward to. I don't ever remember questioning my parents about the monks' lifestyle. It was just who they were, two monks—our uncle and his friend.

The monk who manned the narrow gatehouse at the entrance to the monastery greeted us and announced our arrival. The entrance drive into the abbey boasted towering sweet gum trees on both sides. They were so full it was as if a canopy was placed over the road. I remember my father parking, head in, facing a beautiful large stone wall, which at the time appeared ten feet high.

My memory of Uncle Bill and Brother Pat welcoming the family is vague at best, but I vividly recall many interesting aspects of our visits to the abbey. For example, my sisters and mother were only allowed in certain areas of the monastery. Although my siblings and I never comprehended the restrictions at the time, it was not cause for concern. Rather, there was a sense of sibling rivalry that permeated the air. The guys were allowed in, and the girls were not! You'd think that activities for kids would be limited in a monastery, but not with our uncle. Rides on the huge combine with Uncle Bill when he would plow the fields, visits to the Gethsemani bakery where the world-famous fruitcakes are made, and, if Dad permitted, a quick ride on the conveyor belt were some of the activities that *started the day. Swimming in the monastery pond, visiting the farm, driving the pickup truck in the fields, seeing the chapel and the choir, and touring the beautiful white abbey were enough to put four kids sound asleep on the return trip to Louisville. How fortunate we were to experience those things.*

As a child, I always knew that someone "special" had lived in the monastery, but I didn't know too much about this person or who he was. Little did I know he was one of America's most famous monks and philosophers. I also didn't know it at the time, but Uncle Bill was the cook for Father Louis (Thomas Merton). Brother Pat was not only one of Merton's closest friends and advisors, but also his secretary. Upon Merton's death in 1968, Brother Pat became the representative for Merton affairs for the Abbey of Gethsemani. After three decades of leading a cloistered life, Brother Donald left the monastery and the Trappist life of solitude.

What follows is the portrait of Brother Donald Kane; one man, one monk, and one person's call. The Trappists are one of the strictest orders in religious life. Although extremely rigid and pious, their dedication to the Kingdom is not without a few chortles. This reflective account from inside the monastery provides us with an opportunity to explore God's call from a different perspective. This is the story of a very spiritual, prayerful, loving, and gentle person who has spent thirty years behind the walls of the famous Abbey of Gethsemani.

Profile
JERSEY CITY, New Jersey, 1950. As the Korean War dragged on, I knew it wouldn't be long before I was drafted. Before Uncle Sam had the opportunity to draft me into the Army, many of us from the neighborhood decided to enlist while we still had a choice.

My cousin was in the Army and I knew there would be a lot of walking. That wasn't for me, so I chose the Navy. I requested to be assigned to an aircraft carrier overseas. In those days, the government tried to honor your request as best it could.

After a year in Jacksonville, Florida, training for aviation ordnance, I found myself aboard the aircraft carrier *Valley Forge*. I spent the next three years aboard the *Valley Forge*. I really loved that ship and all she had to offer. It was on the *Valley Forge,* in the middle of the Yellow Sea, that I received my vocation. A shipmate of mine, Mark O'Connor, was assigned to the ship as a cleric. Mark was in charge of the chapel, which was for all denominations. One day, I happened to be sitting in the chapel and Mark came in to prepare for Mass. He asked if I would help him ready the chapel for Mass. Fifty years later, Mark and I are still close friends. Today, he is an ordained priest in Garrison, New York.

Knowing the war wouldn't last forever, I began to ruminate about how life would be after the floating city. I was searching for an answer, but found none, so I began to pray about it. As I gazed across the bow of the ship, I saw the beauty of the world, the sea, the sky. You come to realize that someone has to be in charge here, it's about life. So I reflected about God. I concluded, I just wanted to do what God wanted me to do. I was still unsure if God had plans for me to get married. About the same time, my new friend Mark asked if I wanted to go on a retreat together after the war ended. That sounded very appealing, and Mark said he knew "just the place." He suggested we go to a Trappist monastery in Berryville, Virginia. I knew nothing about the life of a Trappist, but when we arrived in Berryville, I knew I was home. It was very austere, and there was absolute silence! While I was there, I was able to speak with a priest, Father Gabriel. I made a general confession to Father Gabriel and from that moment on, I wanted to be a Trappist.

Berryville was a small monastery but very strict. I didn't think I could make it. At the same time, I was reading a book by Thomas Merton called *The Seeds of Contemplation*. Merton was located at the Abbey of Gethsemani, outside of Louisville, Kentucky. I thought, if someone is writing this stuff, something must be going on.

A friend of mine who lived in Kentucky invited me for a visit. I eventually gravitated toward Kentucky. I realized that, although Gethsemani was still a Trappist order, it was much larger than Berryville. I was hoping, in some way, to get lost in the crowd.

When I left Virginia, I went home to be with my father, who was suffering from loneliness. I never told him what my plans were. He knew I had gone on retreat twice before, but he had no inkling of my desire to join. I never would have left for the monastery while my father was still alive, but he died later that year. I arrived at Gethsemani in December of 1955. Prior to arriving in Kentucky, I gave everything I had to my Aunt Sadie and Uncle George, and I gave my car to a friend of mine. Abbot Dom James Fox accepted me as a postulant. He was a wonderful man, and a wonderful abbot, and treated all of us as though we were his sons. Dom James was a graduate of the Harvard Business School. He helped put Gethsemani on the map by establishing Gethsemani Farms.

The thought of going to the seminary to become a priest never crossed my mind. I became enamored with the Trappist lifestyle; I fell in love. The farming, the down-to-earth kinds of things, the silence, the middle of the night—it was great, it was new, it was holy, and it was a beautiful thing.

For the first couple of years in Gethsemani, I almost froze to death. We had no heat to speak of, and we really didn't eat

> It wasn't until after a couple of years that I took the three monastic vows: obedience, conversion of manners, and stability.

very much. The morning meal consisted of just a slice or two of bread and coffee. We slept in little cells. A bed consisting of three wooden planks laid next to each other with a straw mattress, a cross, and two holy pictures were all that we had in our cell. A cell was no bigger than a dining room table. It was just long enough to lay down in. Today, however, it's much different.

Monastery life was very rigid. But I enjoyed it. I was comfortable with the lifestyle as soon as I arrived. I was a novice for six years and took simple vows during that time. We were separate from the older monks in the sense that we were still learners of the lifestyle. It wasn't until after a couple of years that I took the three monastic vows: obedience, conversion of manners, and stability. None of the vows were difficult for me to take.

Our only form of communication in the monastery was by sign language. We could speak to the abbot, the priest hearing confessions, and the brother delegating the work, but that was about it. The silence was not difficult at all. It was really a pleasant way to live. One of the brothers used to say, "We love at different levels."

When you're silent, you really get to love people at a different level. It's so deep. You're constantly thinking about God and love and the spiritual angle of things, and you're not distracted by everyone's conversation.

There were hundreds of monks when I first entered. So many, in fact, that some in the community had to sleep in makeshift tents located in the cloister courtyard. Many were studying to become priests. Me, I just enjoyed being a brother.

In the early days, we awoke at 2:00 in the morning. We were already fully dressed because we slept in our clothes. All we had to do was roll out of bed, put on our shoes, wash our faces, and go to church. We prayed the seven offices every day. After Lauds, about sunrise, we would start our work. I spent many years working on the farm. It was probably my favorite job at the monastery. No matter where we were working, when it was time for another office, we stopped what we were doing and prayed where we were.

The fun part of the monastic religious life was the beauty of it and the work involved: working in the fields, going on retreat in the woods in winter, gathering branches and colorful leaves for celebrations, harvesting the crops, caring for each other, witnessing the dawns, visiting the church day and night. The stars, the trees, the horizon, the silence, the prayer, doing the work of God in church or in fields or woods filled me with a sense of joy and awesomeness of the responsibility of living in the liberty and freedom of God. I came to realize that we live by every word from the mouth of God.

There is a sense of discovery to the monastic life as well. Though we, especially those of us in religious life, are caught up in answering the main questions of life (where did we come from, who made us, where are we going, and why are we here), there is a discovery to be made in asking the question of what we are learning. What is Love? What is this "Rule of Saint Benedict" that we live by? After all, we didn't enter monastic life to keep a rule as such. But, as Saint Augustine said, "Such a life and rule is a discipline of human culture and is permeated with the light and truth of God, and the knowledge and love of God!" This discipline of human culture (one of many) points out to us God's incarnational love. And this dynamic tradition is everyone's, not only monastic life, but yours and mine as well. Truly, the monk is least of all the saints, even in such an austere style of life as the monastery.

When I first entered in 1955, silence was a rule, not a vow. This really helped everyone "be together" yet alone with God as they say. Being together helps, but sometimes it hinders. For a period of time, one of my jobs was cooking for the other monks. It was my least favorite job in the monastery, but nonetheless it was an important one.

In a monastic's life, it was the little things that happened in which one found humor. As the cook, I needed supplies to feed three hundred monks. One time, I filled my rickety old wagon with supplies. As I was walking back to the main building, I realized I had to take my cargo of food down a bumpy, rocky, sloped entrance to the kitchen. Enlisting help to negotiate the slope was imperative, or my supplies would spill. One of the brothers, who had an Irish smile of curiosity, came and offered to help. I held the handle up front and Brother took up the rear. But instead of holding the cart back, he gave it a push. My hands slipped from the handle. I tried to grab it back, but the heavy wagon pushed me right through the kitchen door. My robe got caught in the wheels and ripped. Yes, the rewards of being together were great, as was evidenced by the big smile on Brother's face.

Feast days were always fun in the monastery. They were special days on which we could enjoy a beer or a glass of wine. Usually we would take just one, but it tasted so good, that sometimes I would pour one into my metal cup and take another one with me on a walk. Once a brother working in the bakery dipped into the bourbon that we used for fruitcakes. He was a novice and his father was coming to visit, so he decided to give him a gift. He took a whole box of cherries and inoculated them with bourbon.

We had an infirmary at the monastery as well. With our special care, the older monks resided and yet lived the rule of life as best they could. I went there just because. The infirmary chapel faced east and the sun came up each day, shining through the large Linden tree outside, filling the chapel with life and light. The bees awoke and filled the tree with a buzz. And at the window sat old Brother John. I loved to watch Brother John. He just sat there tilling his beads and swinging his legs. He couldn't walk very well and he had a little tune he liked to whistle as he watched the day and the bees and life arise. It was a joy for me to see him there. The memories will last a lifetime. Whenever I felt down, just thinking of Old Brother John whistling and tilling his beads made me happy.

Then there was old Father Steven. He resided in the infirmary as well. The infirmary was a wealth of healing grace. Old Father Steve had a hunched back and a game leg. His bad leg made him lumber down the cloister "like a train," Thomas Merton would say.

Father Steve said Mass every morning in the chapel of the infirmary by himself. There was no schedule for him. If we were lucky, we would attend his Mass. He had white hair and a white beard and he told me he always wanted to be a Carthusian, but the pope would not let him. "Stay where you are," the pope would say. Father Steve had a smile from ear to ear; a smile bespeaking mischief. His hands and knuckles were enlarged from rheumatism and his long fingers were always pointed (as I always thought) to graces yet unseen. When Father Steve gave out Communion at one end of the altar, he would lean on one elbow and with a big grin would offer you the Body of Christ. "Body of Christ," he would say, smiling. To this day, those memories are a wonderful grace.

I also did the cooking in the infirmary, not just for Brother John and Father Steve, but for many of the monks, including Thomas Merton. Merton had a bad back, so he was put on a special diet.

Father Steve had a little garden by the cloister wall. He grew flowers of all kinds. He would till the ground and work the soil and he'd smile and wave his long-fingered hands at me when I walked past him. Father Steve gave a bouquet of flowers to every monk who had family visiting. He always loved to be in his garden. When I was cooking, he would come to me before dinner, lumbering along, waving his hands, smiling his mischievous grin, and ask, "Instead of my chicken, can I have a piece of cheese to take with me?" How could I resist, even though it was Sunday meal? Later, I'd walk by Steve and receive a rewarding mischievous grin from a happy monk. These kinds of memories are an everlasting grace.

> On December 10, 1968, the Abbey of Gethsemani forever changed.

On December 10, 1968, the Abbey of Gethsemani forever changed. It was 12:30 P.M. We were in the refectory having lunch when Father Flavian tapped his tin cup with a fork to get our attention. "Father Louis has died! He was electrocuted in Bangkok!" I believe those were the only words spoken by Father Flavian when he announced Thomas Merton's passing. "Oh God!" I thought. We almost fell over. Everything was a blur. We were in shock and our community was stunned. I couldn't finish eating, and I don't remember what I did next.

Upon my arrival at Gethsemani, Thomas Merton (Father Louis) was the novice master. He would give talks to the young novices every day to help them through the monastic life. Merton's books provided not only an income for the monastery, but postulants as well. Many joined the monastery because of Thomas Merton's books. To a degree, that's what led me to Gethsemani. Merton's books made not only Gethsemani well known, but all monasteries. He had tremendous character and was very contemplative. It was really beautiful to watch him whenever he walked into the cloister. He always smiled, but never said a word. He used no hand gestures. But he had a style about him. He walked into the cloister like something was really going on in life. He'd look at you with his eyes and you knew he was saying, "What have you discovered today?" He'd just lean back and smile at you when you walked by. I would occasionally see him outside working with the novices. Every time I went out for hay, he was always trying to get the novices to get their work done correctly. Once in a while, he'd make me laugh. As everyone else was working, he'd take a break and sit on a bail of hay. Every so often, I would go to his hermitage and take care of the bushes and trees. Once, as he was walking along reading, he called me "Ave," as in "Ave, Maria" or "Hail." I never forgot it.

In the years before Merton, the Cistercian life of a Trappist was very austere. Their heads were down, and they were quiet and humble with their noses to the grindstone. Thomas Merton got the place recognized with his autobiography. Not just Gethsemani, but the whole Cistercian order. The Trappists throughout the world woke up to sunshine. The world knew us, and we knew ourselves! That's the way he was. Whether walking in the cloister or outside, he was very cheerful. There was never any downcast or grumpiness about him. He was always very upbeat.

I believe the last time I saw Father Louie was after lunch one day, in November of 1968, just before he departed for the Orient. Merton didn't want to be treated like anyone special in the monastery. He was a monk, humble in his ways, just like the rest of us. Father Louie was buried in the Gethsemani cemetery. He has a plain white cross that bears his priestly name, "Father Louis." That's the way he would have wanted it to be.

> To live
> the life
> of a religious
> is to live
> a beautiful life.

The life of a monk, or the lives of those with a family, are gifts given by God. The dynamics of monastic life, especially contemplative life, can be for everyone. Those who come to a monastery see it and come to know it as their own. The monk is a person working out the dynamic of nature and grace in a life of praise before God. That's all that it is, and that's everything that it is.

The daily workings of this dynamic are guided and directed in many different religious orders in many different ways. In the contemplative life, prayer, reading, and labor nourish the soul of the monk. In other orders, prayer, teaching, preaching, and caring for the sick and dying take on a more active part in the world. Yet it all comes down to the same thing. The person doing the work is working out his or her own dynamic of nature and grace before God, and in the love of God.

As an observer seeing the monks in choir, one can tell immediately that human nature cannot be denied. Old and young, weak and hearty, energetic and slow, strong and tall, short and fat, awake or sleeping (yes, sleeping), you name it, we see ourselves.

On the invisible side, monks are humorous, silent, loving, caring, hardworking, fun-loving, serious in their quest, and sharing whenever possible of what they have and what they know to be the love of God.

With all that combined, nature and grace is the soil on which a happy and spiritual life is built. The life of a monk is for beginners and its dynamic dimensions are everyone's, even in the more intense vocations of life where there is love of God and neighbor. Each one of us can truly find the person we are when we respond to God's grace.

To live the life of a religious is to live a beautiful life.

6

"Be careful, o priest, what you ask for. You might get it."

Thank you, God

IS THERE a particular story you remember from one of your priests' homilies that continues to inspire you? Do you know someone who has the necessary qualities needed to become a priest?

NO BOOK on priests would be complete without a chapter on the inspirational events that have taken place throughout their life ministries. I believe many of the stories in this chapter truly show how fortunate a priest is to share so intimately in the lives of his parishioners. Not only does the priest touch the hearts of his people, but the people can touch the heart of their priest.

I would speculate that there is not a priest working today who cannot share a touching story. The stories that have been submitted are splendid examples of how God's grace establishes a foothold on our very soul. They enable us to explore more personally what God means to us on an individual basis. They focus our thoughts on what is really important in our own everyday lives.

And they are as varied as the priests who responded, and once again demonstrate the humanity, the dedication, and the goodness of the men we call "Father."

I WAS ORDAINED about a year or less when a remarkable event took place. It was my birthday, and some friends in the parish invited me over to their home for a little birthday party: cake and candles and the whole nine yards. I was just getting ready to leave for the party when the phone rang. I debated whether to answer it or not, but I decided I had better check it out.

It turned out to be the night nurse from a local nursing home. She told me there was a resident in the home who had slipped into a coma earlier that day, his daughter was with him and she had requested a priest. The nurse apologized for calling our rectory, but the chaplain had left earlier that day on an overnight trip and so she called me.

I asked if the man had been anointed recently, and she said that he had indeed been anointed two weeks ago, but that was before his latest setback. I said that would probably be okay, but she went on to say that the daughter was pretty upset, and would really like for her dad to receive the sacraments. I said okay, reluctantly.

I called my friends to say I was going to be a little late, but to hold the cake, I would be over as soon as I could. I drove over to the nursing home, met the nurse, and she took me to see the gentleman.

It was as I suspected. He was lying in bed, breathing heavily and unconscious. His daughter was very grateful for me coming over and I could tell she had been crying. I intended to make this as brief as possible, so I said a few prayers, anointed the man with the Holy Oil, and then invited the nurse and the daughter to pray the Our Father with me.

We started the prayer, "Our Father, who art in heaven, hallowed be thy name. Thy kingdom come, thy will be done on earth as it is in heaven." When we got to this part, the man's eyes opened up, and he joined us. "Give us this day our daily bread and forgive us our trespasses, as we forgive those who trespass against us."

By this point we had stopped our words, our jaws dropped, and our eyes bugged out. He completed the prayer, "And lead us not into temptation, but deliver us from evil. Amen." The nurse went over to him, took some vitals, and smiled and said, "Welcome back, Mr. Hanlon." He looked up and said, "Hi, Father. Hi, Honey."

The nurse was amazed, the daughter was beside herself. She said, "Thank you, Father, thank you!" I said, "It wasn't me. It normally doesn't work this way. The people usually stay down after I anoint them." Regardless, it was a very special moment.

After a few moments, as we were walking down the corridor to the door, the daughter spoke up. She said, "I'm very grateful! I know it was an imposition to ask you to come on such short notice. But it was important, because you see, today is my father's birthday!" I said, "No way, it's my birthday, too." She said, "No way!"

I took out my driver's license and showed her the proof. We both looked at each other in silence. God had made his point. I went over there feeling put-upon. I was being deprived of my little party, but God clearly had other plans for me. He gave me a wake-up call to remind me of who and what I am. I truly believe he did this to shake me into a right frame of mind when I'm privileged to be his instrument.

This is a true story. It remains one of the most remarkable events in my twenty-two years as a priest.

> *† Father Dennis R. Stehly*
> *Archdiocese of St. Louis*

IT WAS IN SUISUN CITY in northern California that my story begins. It was a cool Saturday morning and I was visiting an engaged couple. I was helping them with the documents that they needed so that they could marry in the Catholic church.

As I left their house, I saw a lady next door who was sweeping the sidewalk. She turned to me and called, "Are you a Catholic priest?" When I answered that I was, she said, "Could you please go see a lady who is very ill? She wants very much to see a priest."

I said that I would be glad to see her. But when I asked for the name and address, the lady said, "I do not know her name for sure, it could be Rosa, and I do not know where she lives. I do know that she is Italian and married to a Spaniard and that she is paralyzed from the waist down. Then she pointed to the northeast, toward Fairfield, where Travis Air Force Base is located. The lady said, "She lives that way."

I responded, "I'll find her." I remember I did not feel any frustration or doubt.

I drove in the direction she had indicated. I was driving just under an hour when I saw that I was getting closer to Travis Air Force Base. I saw houses everywhere, and had no idea which one was her home. Then something told me to park near a field where there were some homes. I thought that I would go from house to house to ask if anyone knew the lady.

As I approached the first house, something told me to go to the third house instead. I knocked at the front door. No one answered. I decided then to go to the back of the house where I climbed up some stairs and knocked again. I heard a shuffling on the steps.

A man about sixty or so (I was twenty-seven at the time) opened the door and greeted me in Spanish. From his accent I knew that he was Spanish. When I asked him if he knew a lady named Rosa who was paralyzed from the waist down, he smiled and said, "Yes, she is my wife. We have been waiting for you!"

I was not at all surprised. It all seemed so natural. When Rosa saw me she exclaimed in Italian that I was an angel from heaven. With my limited Italian we did manage to talk a bit. She was very happy. I returned a few days later to offer Mass in her home.

Some three months later someone called to let me know that she was dying in a Fairfield hospital. I drove quickly to the hospital to see her. When she saw me, she smiled. Only a few minutes later she died.

I decided to drive to her husband's home to let him know that she had died. Wouldn't you know it, I could not find the house. Then I did feel frustrated. I could not find the house at all.

Later that evening when I returned to the rectory in Stockton, I related this incident to an elderly priest. When I told him that I could not find the house to tell the husband about his wife's death, the priest simply said, "That was not in God's plan."

† Father Antonio A. Sotelo
Diocese of Phoenix

155

MY FIRST ASSIGNMENT was at a fairly large church, Christ the King, in Yonkers, New York. The pastor and I didn't really get along too well. It seemed that no matter what I did, I couldn't please him. I was fresh out of the seminary, and I would have done just about anything to please my pastor.

He was an older man, so I took that into consideration. By the end of my first year I still had had no luck in pleasing him. It was getting so bad that I almost put in for a transfer. I went on a week long vacation and when I returned, the pastor told me he was going to the hospital. No big deal, I thought. Possibly it was just a sick call or he wanted to visit a friend. Later that night, the phone rang. It was the pastor telling me that the doctor wanted to keep him in the hospital for a couple of days, and that he had actually gone in for a check up.

That night they operated on him. I found out the next morning that he had terminal cancer. He came back to the rectory where he stayed for the next seven months. It was very tough for him. He had been at Christ the King for forty years. To have some young guy come in and take over all the responsibility was tough. He was also in a great deal of pain. I watched him go downhill every day.

Months later, the pastor was in Saint John's Hospital. Our relationship hadn't improved at all. On Easter Sunday I was driving home to spend the day with my family. On the way there, I drove right past the hospital. Even though the pastor and I didn't see eye to eye, he was still a brother priest, and pastor of our church. I stopped the car, turned around, and went to visit him.

I got to his hospital room and he was lying on his side. We began to talk a little bit and the pastor was upset that this illness had hit him like this. He knew he was dying. I had to be on my way, but I felt that I wanted to apologize to him. I told him, "Monsignor, I would like to apologize to you for the tough times that we had together in the past and that I care about you very much. And I wish you weren't going through this!"

The Monsignor was in so much pain that he really couldn't talk very well. When I told him how sorry I was for everything, he turned his head toward me and nodded, as if to say he was sorry, too.

That evening, after I left, Monsignor slipped into a coma. He passed away two days later. I was so very thankful I stopped by to make peace with him. To me, it's a wonderful example of the power of the priesthood and the power of forgiveness. It wiped away all the past anger that had been built up!

I thank God I stopped to say I was sorry.

† Father William J. Damroth III
Archdiocese of New York

ABOUT EIGHTEEN MONTHS after I baptized their fifth child, Ann had a stroke. Her husband asked me if I could be there when he would have to announce her death to their children. Three weeks later, at about 7:30 on a Sunday morning, the phone rang and he informed me she had died during the night. I was there at 7:45. He sat his four older children on the couch and handed me the youngest to hold. He took a chair to speak to his children.

When the older children started crying, I could feel the little one react in my arms. It was a sad funeral. Ten months later, the recent young widower married his high school sweetheart, and she promised to help raise his children. That promise was touchingly made after the marriage vows.

Last week the phone rang, and I was asked to witness the marriage of the little one whom I held so sadly in my arms twenty-five years ago. She looks just like her mom, and when she ran into my arms the memories of long ago came rushing back in all their clarity, starkness, and pathos.

It still wrings my heart and brings a tear to my eye.

† Father C. Peter Dumont
Diocese of Manchester

I WAS A MISSIONARY in the country of Zambia, which is located in Africa, from 1972 to 1980.

One day I started driving from my main post along a dirt road that ran through a dense forest, heading to a mission outpost station where I was to say Mass. I was dressed in civilian clothing.

Suddenly, as if from nowhere, I was surrounded by a massive contingent of Freedom Fighters, two of whom placed their guns none too gently against both sides of my upper neck, while others bombarded me with rapid questions, and others kicked me. How can I describe the terror? I have never found adequate words.

All my life swirled before me. Did God want me to die so soon? Would this dreadful moment ever pass? People were waiting for me at Mass. I was sweating and shaking and speechless! I was terrified, experiencing a myriad of emotions!

Suddenly, I knew not from where, a woman appeared, her two arms extended, and, attempting to push the men away from me, she shouted to them, repeating that I was a priest.

The pressure of the gun against my neck eased. I was spent. Divine Intervention! These were Freedom Fighters from Rhodesia, now known as Zimbabwe. They possibly thought I was a spy for the Rhodesian Ian Smith government.

This event comes to mind with great frequency, and so often, along with the flashback, I feel the terror, the relief, and the gratitude. Divine Intervention!

God evidently has more things for me to do.

† Father Joseph Parel
Archdiocese of Hartford

I AM A NATIVE of India and a priest of forty years. I came to the United States in 1990 and first landed in San Francisco. When I came out of the airport I had two big suitcases and a briefcase. I was looking for someone to help me carry my bags to a taxi. Then I found a man holding a placard with my name on it. I assumed he was the one the parish had sent to pick me up and take me back to the church.

He was dressed shabbily and had a thick mustache. With his size and structure, and loose tee shirt, I really thought he must be either a porter or a taxi driver sent from the church.

I gave him a strong order to put my luggage in the car and he readily obeyed. Only on my way to the church did I realize that the man, my taxi driver, was a provincial (a bishop) where I was to be an associate pastor.

† Father Berchmans Konnully
Diocese of Bismarck

ONCE I WAS HELPING to lead a retreat for married couples. We had a special time to celebrate the sacrament of Reconciliation. A lady came into my Reconciliation room and chose to celebrate the sacrament in a confidential way (not face to face).

About halfway through, she told me she was going to have a baby. Not knowing who she was, I wanted to deal with her pregnancy in a respectful way.

I knew everyone on the retreat was married. In order to find out more and why she was mentioning it in the confessional, I asked her if her husband knew about the pregnancy. She said "yes," so I asked her why she was mentioning it now. She said, "I am going to have the baby right now!"

This startled me somewhat and I told her, "We obviously cannot keep this under seal."

There was a great deal of excitement as we brought her to her room and called a doctor.

She ultimately ended up giving birth two days later, but it was an exciting retreat nonetheless.

† Anonymous

✝

I WAS BORN IN JULY 1937, of Irish and Sicilian descent, the youngest of three boys. I attended a coinstitutional grade school where not only were the boys and girls separated in the classroom, but even our playgrounds were on opposite sides of the school.

After graduation in 1951, I attended a high school preparatory seminary six hundred miles from home. After the all-boys' high school seminary, I entered a major seminary. From 1955 to 1964 seminaries were truly seed beds with no such thing as a home visit and very little contact with the outside world. My first assignment found me teaching in seminaries, again in the unreal world far from any contact with the opposite sex.

The point? For the whole of my life I could hardly say the word "woman" without blushing, but the year 1975 found me living with fifty women and attending Texas Women's University in Denton, Texas.

I went back to school in 1975. And from 1975 to 1980 I was resident chaplain to the School Sisters of Notre Dame at their Motherhouse in Irving, Texas. The post-conciliar years were tumultuous for the church. Seemingly, John XXIII's challenge to read the signs of the times proved too much for many of the churchmen, but the sisters took the call to renewal in stride.

It was in the convent where I learned community. It was in that same convent where I had my social consciousness raised. It was there that I experienced a true worshiping community. I was made aware of what to boycott and why. It was the first time I heard that caring for the environment was a moral issue. It was also there that I regained an appreciation for my priesthood that I had lost somewhere along the way.

Needless to say, I was introduced to feminist theology and its correlative, liberation theology. Both were sure a far cry from the white, male, privileged, western European theology I was exposed to in my seminary days. Herve and Noldin were replaced by Elizabeth A. Johnson and Gustavo Gutierrez.

It was in those "formative years" that I really grew into my priesthood. There was a man at the turn of the last century who was head of the patent office in Washington, D.C., who wanted to close the patent office down because he thought everything that was to be invented had already been invented. No prophet he! My greatest fear is that I will be like the poor sap with no vision and no soul.

Because my awareness had been raised by faithful and dedicated churchwomen, I now refuse to believe that the church has progressed as far as it can. I refuse to believe that John Paul II or all his successors will have said the last word.

I refuse to be fixated at any stage in church history, be it the early church, the Middle Ages, the Renaissance, the 1950s, or the 2000s. The Holy Spirit doesn't sleep.

There's a hymn by Darryl Ducote which takes us through salvation history with the response being, "All that we can offer you is thanks." This is my offering to the School Sisters of Notre Dame and to all the women in our church who have not given up hope and will march fearlessly into the twenty-first century working for a collaborative and inclusive church.

† Father August A. Melito
Diocese of Dallas

✝

I'M A FATHER and a "father." In 1970, I was in Vietnam. I was flying up and down the border saying Mass for the Special Forces and sometimes taking cover from rocket attacks. The rocket attacks were frequent. You lived with the feeling that any day you would be overrun.

After many visits to the Catholic orphanage, I decided to adopt two children, Vu Dinh Son and his little sister Vu Thi Thuy, now called Peter and Maria. Once back home, I had to get used to being a "father."

I can remember the time when I scraped pork chops off the kitchen ceiling. Somehow, the water evaporated and the cooker blew apart. Then there was the time I sewed myself to the sewing machine. Peter wanted me to put some patches on his jacket, and I didn't realize it while I was sewing, but somehow my sleeve went where it shouldn't have, and I sewed my sleeve to his jacket.

Maria has plenty of curiosity and spunk. Once she walked up to Cardinal Terence Cooke when I was at their base in Panama and demanded to know why girls couldn't serve Mass.

† Father James E. Somma
Diocese of Pittsburgh

MANY YEARS AGO, I had another job in our parish in addition to my regular priestly duties. I had to get the pigeons under control! It started becoming very troublesome and downright dangerous to stand on the front steps of the church. The facade of the church, which was repointed, was becoming encrusted with pigeon droppings.

The birds had taken over the rose window and I expected to see a small sign appear up there (in Pigeon English, of course) reading "Home Sweet Home!"

When I saw feathers waltzing down the center aisle of the church one Sunday, I knew it was time to try some new tactics.

I had posted rubber owls on the roof and in the tower. I had rubber snakes in all the drain pipes, but the pigeon "IQ" seemed to be on the rise. We had to take a more devious route. Thus, "Pigeon Control" was underway. I told my parishioners to move quickly from the top front step into the vestibule.

The "coif" they saved may be their own!

A year or two after our pigeon problem, a parishioner sent me a reflection titled "The Perfect Pastor." I'm sure this is appropriate for all parish priests.

THE PERFECT PASTOR

Results of a computerized survey indicate that the perfect pastor preaches exactly fifteen minutes and always has the people "out" in half an hour. He condemns sin, but never embarrasses anyone. He works from 8:00 A.M. until midnight and is also the janitor.

He keeps the parish property in tip-top shape, gives all his employees a just wage, balances the books with ease, but never mentions money except to condemn it as the root of all evil.

He makes sixty dollars a week, wears good clothes, drives a new car, and gives fifty dollars a week to the poor. He is twenty-eight years old and has been preaching for twenty-five years, is wonderfully gentle and handsome, loves to work with teenagers, and spends countless hours with the elderly.

He is at all the Sunday Masses, baptizes and marries in the afternoon with love and devotion, cheers on the parish basketball teams later in the day—in between visits to the sick and shut-ins.

He is present at the evening parental meetings and charms the teenagers at the CYO meeting, yet finds the time to while away a pleasant evening playing Bingo in the parish hall. He makes fifteen calls daily on parish families, shut-ins, and hospital patients, and is always in his office when needed.

If your pastor does not measure up, simply send this letter to six other parishes that are tired of their pastors, too. Then bundle up your pastor and send him to the church at the top of the list. In one week you will receive 1,643 pastors. One of them should be perfect!

> † *Father Charles E. Maher*
> *Diocese of Providence*

FOUR YEARS after my ordination, I was made pastor of Kodiak Island, the second-largest island in the United States after Hawaii. Six years later I was transferred to a large Anchorage parish and for the past seven years I have been here in Soldotna on the beautiful Keni River.

If you happen to be worshiping at Our Lady of Perpetual Help between Memorial Day and Labor Day you might hear me say at announcement time, "Any folks want to go rafting with me after Sunday Mass?"

Most Sunday afternoons, I take up to six people on a ten-mile raft trip in the mountainous upper section of the Kenai. Usually, the guests provide a nice lunch for the rower priest—me!

I've found that if I invite the grandmothers, the lunches are really spectacular—something about getting to heaven by feeding Father.

So come worship with us, and bring lunch for the raft trip.

† Father Richard D. Tero
Archdiocese of Anchorage

I WAS ORDAINED MAY 23, 1961. I became convinced at some point in my priesthood that an essential ingredient to being a happy priest is a sense of humor. Somewhere along the line I developed the habit of telling a joke or two before beginning the homily. Whenever I miss telling one or two a week, I am gently reminded. People remember (and retell) my jokes. My homilies? Who knows?

† Father Joel S. Bladt, S.T.
Diocese of Savannah

FOR SEVEN YEARS I was a missionary in Bolivia, South America. I went to the Maryknoll language school in the beautiful city of Cochabamba. The story was told there of a missioner (not me) who went to the marketplace in Cochabamba while in language school.

In broken Spanish he tried to ask for a "chullu" (pronounced chew you), which is like a wool stocking cap with ear flaps and is made by Bolivian Indians. They are very useful during cold weather, especially on the altiplano.

Instead, the priest mistakenly asked for a "chola," which is an Indian woman.

The vendor realized that his Spanish was not very good so she tried and tried to explain to him that he simply could not purchase a "chola," but the priest persisted.

Finally, she asked him why he wanted to purchase this item. He explained that he wanted the chola to keep him warm at night!

The moral of the story is:

Be careful, o priest, what you ask for; you just might get it.

† Father James J. Foster
Archdiocese of St. Louis

Hilton L. Rivet, S.J.

Born IN NEW ORLEANS, Louisiana, on August 21, 1922, he grew up in a wealthy home, the son of a prominent lawyer. As most of the world struggled to get by, he was surrounded with vacation homes, automobiles, and the finest schools.

WHY DID HE give up a life that most people could only dream about? Leaving his longtime sweetheart and opulent surroundings, he entered the seminary on September 21, 1941, on a thirteen-year quest to become a Jesuit priest.

*As he approaches his eightieth birthday, Father Hilton
Rivet still serves as pastor of Immaculate Conception Church in
Baton Rouge, Louisiana. He is one of a handful of white
people living in an African-American community in the deep
south.*

*Hilton Rivet is an inspiring man. He has been fortunate to
experience church and societal changes throughout his forty-
seven-year ministry. This is his story.*

Profile

MY VOCATION was most unusual.
Typically, when someone entered the seminary in the 1930s or
1940s, they did so early on in their schooling. It was not
unusual for young boys to enter the minor seminary as early as
the eighth grade. Many entered directly out of high school. For
me, the road to priesthood began as I was about to enter my
junior year at Loyola University.

Entering the seminary as an "old" guy and growing up in
an affluent family in the segregated south seem contradictory to
where I am today. But God knew what he was doing.

Never in my life did I feel compelled to respond to the nuns
who used to ask, "So how many of you are going to be priests?"
In grammar school, all the boys would dutifully put up their
hands, but of course they never did anything about it. I had no
inclinations toward the priesthood whatsoever.

In July of 1941, I went on a retreat just as I finished my
second year of college at Loyola. I only went there because my
father used to go every year. It surely wasn't because I was
pious or anything like that, I guess he persuaded me by his
example to go and see what it was all about. So off I went. At
that time, though, I was very much enamored of a young lady
who I had been going with for five years. Her name was Judy.

During the retreat, we were very much alone. We didn't talk to anybody. In every retreatant's room there was a Bible. Even though I went to Catholic school my entire life, I knew nothing about the Bible. I just opened it to the New Testament to see what it was all about and began to read this delightful story about a rich young man who was invited by

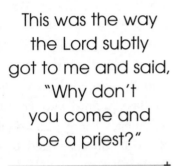

This was the way the Lord subtly got to me and said, "Why don't you come and be a priest?"

Jesus to come and follow him. But the man couldn't follow Jesus. He couldn't leave all that "stuff" behind because he was so materialistic. Now, I could identify with that completely because I was a rich young man. My father was a very prominent and successful lawyer. We lived in a very fancy part of town in the nicest area of New Orleans—it was called the Silk Stocking.

As I was reading this story, I identified with it thoroughly. This was my life! This was the way the Lord subtly got to me and said, "Why don't you come and be a priest?" When the thought came into my mind I dismissed it immediately. This was not for me! So I finished the retreat with that little thought tucked away.

Afterward, I went back home and the thought would come and bring a certain level of peace and happiness. I thought of it as kind of a challenge. Again, I would dismiss it as ridiculous.

In the 1930s and 1940s, just getting by was considered a success. Our family had a summer home on the Gulf Coast, in Mississippi, that's how wealthy we were. I remember asking my mother if I could borrow her car. In those days youngsters didn't have cars. I told her I wanted to borrow the car to go back to New Orleans and see Judy. Everybody loved Judy, but

169

I didn't go to see her. I was going to New Orleans to talk with somebody, anybody, about this nagging thought of becoming a priest. At the time, the provincial lived at our Jesuit high-school residence in New Orleans. I continued to drive round and round the block. I didn't want to get out of the car. I finally parked the car and went in, but I chickened out at the last minute and could not bring myself to ask for the provincial. There was an elderly priest who was an old friend of the family that resided there as well. His name was Father Foulkes.

I finally arrived at the front door of the residence and asked the receptionist if I could speak with Father Foulkes. Father Foulkes was almost eighty years old and talked through his nose. He came down the stairs and greeted me in his whiny, nasal voice. "My son, what are you doing here?" I sat down with him and shared the story of how I had this thought of becoming a priest. He listened very attentively and said, "Well, let me tell you: a young lady came to see me one time and said she thought she wanted to be a nun. I told her that if in one month she hadn't made up her mind, then she should forget it. She's married today and has five children." I was devastated! He didn't give me any encouragement. So I left, still in a quandary, and went back home.

The thought continued to nag me. Up to that point in my life, I only knew Jesuit priests. As a youngster, I went to a Jesuit grammar school. In my later years I went to a Jesuit high school, and Loyola University was just a block from where we lived. The Jesuits were part and parcel of my youth.

I felt bad about lying to my mother to use the car, but I wasn't comfortable telling anybody about my thoughts. You see, I was a "big shot" at Loyola. I had been president of my freshman and sophomore classes and was starting my junior year as president of my class. I knew I was a hotshot and I loved being one! I was a proud, arrogant kid! I knew if I told anyone they would have laughed.

Two weeks later, the thoughts kept coming and I went back to my mother. "Mom, I'd like to go see Judy again." "Oh fine," she said, and lent me the car. This time, as I approached the residence, I did have the courage to ask for the provincial. He, too, knew my father well. When I went to meet him, he already knew my background and qualifications. I told him my thoughts and he said, "All right, the first class is already underway, but I can get you in the September 21 class." I told him that would be fine. That left me with only a month before I departed for the seminary.

I remember it very well. I had to tell my mother because, after all, she had to pack a trunk for me. I was sitting on the front porch of our beautiful home rocking in a chair with my mother, something I rarely did. She was suspicious right off the bat. I never sat down and waited for Daddy to come home. Dinner was always promptly at 6:00 P.M. I said, "Momma, I want to tell you something."

"What's that, Hilton?" she asked.

"I'm gonna be a priest." She stopped rocking, paused and scolded me, "You're not to kid that way, Hilton!"

"Momma, I'm gonna be a Jesuit."

"Hilton, God's gonna punish you for talkin' that way!"

"Momma, I really am! I am leaving on September 21."

I told her about meeting the provincial and what the plans were. When she finally realized I was serious, she smiled and began to cry. But I told her she couldn't tell anybody. "Don't even tell Daddy, I'll tell him."

My father was a very formal man, very distant from us. That's the way fathers were in those days. They provided for all our needs, but were not emotionally there for us. In keeping with our formal relationship, I went down to see him in his office. I said, "Daddy, I just wanted to drop in and tell you that I am leaving on September 21 to become a Jesuit priest." He looked up and without any emotion or hesitation said, "Well, that's very fine. I have a great esteem for the Jesuits. They're wonderful people. You'll get a good education. If you decide it's not for you, come on home and we'll welcome you back." I knew my mother must have told him the way he reacted. I asked him not to tell anyone.

I didn't tell anyone until a day or two before I left. When I finally told my brother he was incensed. We were very close and he was insulted he wasn't informed earlier. On the morning of my departure I went to Loyola to tell people what I was doing. No one would believe me. On the way to the seminary, we stopped to see my aunt. When I told her she didn't believe me either. I never did tell Judy what my plans were. I just left without telling her or saying goodbye. I knew that if Judy asked me not to go, I would have changed my mind as quick as you can snap your finger. That's how much she meant to me. I really loved her and it was difficult to leave her, but I had to go.

Many years later, when I became pastor of the very church I grew up in, I had to preside over Judy's funeral. She had gone on to get married and have five kids. When Judy became sick and lay dying in her hospital bed, she looked at me and said, "Hilton, I love you!" I told her I loved her too. I still have very warm feelings for Judy. In the novitiate, about six months after I was there, I had a dream about Judy and it was so real. I believe it was a test of sorts. I began to miss her so much. Despite that very real dream about her, I stayed.

It wasn't really difficult for me to leave my affluent lifestyle. One day I was a city boy and the next day I was planting potatoes in the field like a farmer. Nothing stopped me from doing something once I made up my mind. Even though I was very, very materialistic and I had done so many of those things that wealthy people could do, the seminary's spartan lifestyle was a wonderful experience! I was eager and enthusiastic in the seminary. If my novice master had told me to stand on my head for an hour and then make three turns coming down, I would have done it.

I remember what really set my course as a Jesuit. During the novitiate, I was talking with the novice master and telling him how much I missed Judy. For the first time I began to question my vocation. He said, "Hilton, make no mistake about it, you do have a vocation as a Jesuit priest."

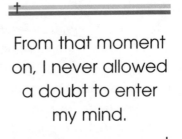

From that moment on, I never allowed a doubt to enter my mind.

From that moment on, I never allowed a doubt to enter my mind. My vocation was a lightning-like thing.

Upon reflection, the seminary was not a real rigid experience. I chose not to think of it as being rigid, even though it really was. Once I accepted the rigidity of the Jesuits I accepted the rigidity as part of the program. It was an accepted normalcy. It was the steady diet.

I did have one expectation when I left the seminary. I had hoped to be like a priest who had had a great influence on me. His name was Father Daniel Lord and he was located in Saint Louis. I would see him in the summer when I would go to a workshop called The Summer School of Catholic Action. I always thought he was a great man. He could play the piano and entertain people and was the type of guy that was influential in bringing the youth into the church. I always wanted to be like him. That really didn't pan out though. In the Jesuits, you go where you're assigned and I was assigned to administration. I always accepted whatever the provincial said.

I was ordained in 1954. My mother and father were very proud of me. I recall my brother telling me, "Hilton, you're so lucky that you don't have any temptations." I responded. "Is that right, Charlie? Do I have a big glob of news for you! Priests have a lot of temptations, maybe even more than the average guy, because there's an enemy around who doesn't like us serving the Lord."

My first assignment was at Loyola University in New Orleans. They needed someone with a graduate degree in sociology. After teaching at Loyola for a year, I was sent to Spring Hill College in Mobile, Alabama. I was Dean of Students and stayed there for eleven years.

Throughout my priesthood, I've been assigned to various ministries, from chaplain of a prison to a pastorate in many churches. I think that what I bring to my ministry is a talent for preaching and presenting the Good News clearly. I enjoy teaching for the same reason. I also enjoy the administration side of being a priest. The secret is to not try to do it all yourself. But always know what's going on and always have the last word.

> I would tell
> a young man
> considering the
> priesthood that
> it's tough, but if
> you like challenges
> it's for you.

The Mass is the high point of my existence. I say Mass every day and that intimacy with the Lord is always the high point of life. Unless a priest has a very intimate, personal love for Jesus Christ (and, of course, for his mother, too), he ain't gonna make it. Life is going to be difficult. Especially in the world that we live in today. You're going to be challenged in different directions. Unless Jesus comes through as the guy who really has it all together, and as the one who we are really serving, the rest of it doesn't make sense.

I would tell a young man considering the priesthood that it's tough, but if you like challenges it's for you. I believe we are selling the youth of today short if we think that they refuse to accept challenges. I think the biggest challenge we have today is that families don't support the idea of their sons going off and becoming priests. I think it's very common in today's society.

Many people think that if priests were allowed to marry, then there would be more clergy. Well, I don't buy it! I think celibacy is the jewel of the church. Those who are priests can appreciate it, except for the disgruntled ones. Some priests have said, "If I had a wife it wouldn't be this tough." Well, hell, they don't know what they're talking about! One of the things a priest sees is the awful tension, stresses, strains, and even hatreds that can sometimes exist within a marriage. When you deal with that over and over again, you realize that marriage is not paradise. I believe priests tend to get the issue of marriage and "loneliness" confused. Priests can become lonely. But then again, doesn't everyone from time to time? Jesuits are lucky in that regard. We have fellow Jesuits whom we live with in community, whom we share our lives with. We tell each other how we feel about things, and we have a lot of fun doing it.

I believe my experience of growing up in a wealthy home and my various ministries have been great assets in my present assignment. I am a white pastor in an African-American church. When I was assigned to this parish in 1994, I welcomed the challenges; I was enthused about coming here.

I came from a white upper-class parish in New Orleans. The parishioners were the hotshots and the wheeler-dealers in the area. They were members of the society group, the kind of group in which I was raised. I knew them well and they knew

175

me, but I don't think they cared for my style of ministry. I would get up in the pulpit and tell them, "You will be relevant in this church in direct proportion to your concern for the poor!" Well, they didn't like hearing that at all.

So when I got to the Black community, it was a delight to be with more authentic Christians! The Black community is more authentic in their relationship with God. It's a joy to preach to the Black community. I have preached in affluent white churches and the members have looked at me with almost contempt, as if to say, "I dare you to say something that you are going to make me affirm." But the Black community is quick to give me an "Amen." If I ask for an "Amen," I get a resounding "Amen." Sometimes I'll say, "That's a mighty weak Amen," and they will respond with a very loud "Amen!" We really have an enthusiastic and inspiring exchange that is just marvelous. It's something we could never have in the White community.

The White community is so damn inhibited! I believe the answer is one word: wealth! Wealth has ruined the White people. It has made them feel that they are superior and that they can't lower themselves and just let their emotions go. It's the arrogance and the pride that comes from wealth. And perhaps part of it is just because they're White. The White people have convinced themselves that they are the so-called superior race. It could very well have been from the slavery days where they found God. When you get to the bottom of the barrel, just like an alcoholic, you're not gonna be any good until things get so bad that you have no place to turn except to God. Then you finally climb out of the barrel. I think that has happened with the White people. It's not just in this country, it's all over the world. France has no one who goes to church anymore.

The African-American community doesn't wear just Christianity on their sleeves, they wear God on their sleeves.

God is very much at home with them and they are very much at home with him. This is true no matter what religion an African-American community practices. As a matter of fact, I don't think being Catholic means that much to the African-American community, it's just being a Christian. Our Catholics (the ones in my church)

Joy is a big thing in the African-American community in reference to God.

can go to a Baptist church and feel totally comfortable. Sure, some would say they need the Eucharist. The Eucharist is central to Catholics. Conversely, Baptists can come to our church and feel totally comfortable. The preaching will make it comfortable for them. It's what you say and how you say it and it's the joy that radiates from the assembly.

Joy is a big thing in the African-American community in reference to God. After Mass is over, it's a delight to see people not running outside to get in their cars like most Catholics do. The African-American community will hang out in the church, talk outside the church, in the foyer, wherever they can. It's wonderful to see.

The music in an African-American Catholic church is altogether different from that in the White Catholic church. I've been pastor of very large affluent White churches where we had a hard time getting fifteen people to sing in the choir. Here at Immaculate Conception, we have four choirs. One choir is unique in that it is a gospel choir. These folks are jammin'! They're really having a good time. Sometimes I have to hold them down and tell them, "This is not a performance, we're worshiping God."

As a pastor, I had the opportunity to learn much about the African-American community. I had to learn. I was fortunate that when I arrived at Immaculate Conception they welcomed me with open arms. It's been a wonderful experience. But there is still work to be done. As my secretary told me, "Father, there's not a day that goes by that I don't know that there is still racial prejudice around." She's right, there is still a lot of it around. The African-American community expresses their feelings, period! They do it in worshiping God, and they do it in everything they do.

What I enjoy most is seeing people develop an appreciation of what being Christian is all about and what being Catholic is all about. I also enjoy getting them involved. I always tell people, "Get involved!" Jesus Christ is really behind it all. It's completely surprising to witness God in the inner worlds of a person. God is very active all the time. Communicating with one person and inspiring another, even admonishing still another. The activity of the divine in the human is absolutely startling. It's a dynamic thing that is operative in everybody. I believe the priest is the only one who has the background to understand what's happening and the willingness to attribute certain things to God where others would dismiss it. God is present though me. Without him, I have no life! Remember the saying, "Get a Life?" You could never say that to a priest in my book. We have the richest possible life that can be imagined! There's nothing like it.

"These are the ordinary saints, the people we know, our relatives, our loved ones."

For All the Saints

During THE FIRST YEARS of my priesthood, the feast of All Saints simply was not a day I anticipated with joy. It usually fell on a weekday and parishioners were not sure of the Mass times, so the phone would ring all day. The crowds of people who came to Mass seemed anything but enthusiastic. Most had either risen early and rushed to church before going to work, or had to catch an evening Mass after they were worn out from a long day on the job.

Furthermore, I wondered why we had to celebrate another feast in honor of all those saints whom we already honored individually on the other days throughout the year. Saints Mary and Joseph, Peter and Paul, and the apostles all had their special feast days, so why such a commotion on November 1?

One day, as I was struggling to prepare a homily for the feast of All Saints, the answer suddenly occurred to me. The church never really intended this to be a day on which to honor all the big saints; rather, this is the day set aside to honor the ordinary saints, the countless millions who lived simple lives like you and me, but who by the grace and mercy of God are now saints in heaven. These are people we knew, our relatives, our loved ones. The feast of All Saints is their feast day!

As I came to this realization, I began to think of some of the many saints whom I have been privileged to know personally. I'd like to tell you about some of them.

THERE IS Saint Ryan Patrick Lenz. Little Ryan was only two years old when he died. An only child, he was his parents' pride and joy, the center of their lives. Ryan was a healthy, normal child, a bundle of energy. When he was suddenly called from this life into eternity, he left his parents, relatives, and friends in a state of shock and grief.

I was out of town at the time of Ryan's death. When I returned several days after the funeral and received the sad news, I went over to visit Ryan's parents and express my condolences. We sat together in the living room which now seemed so empty and reminisced while we looked at Ryan's baby pictures. What an angel he was!

Ryan's dad was a licensed pilot and frequently had taken his wife and son for plane rides. He told how on a recent flight over the city one evening little Ryan had suddenly begun to comprehend the meaning of the words "up" and "down." Suddenly, he realized that those city lights were really way "down" there. After that everything was "up" and "down." Ryan would come running into the house shouting, "Airplane! Airplane!" every time a plane flew over.

Then the grieving parents told me that as the tiny white casket was being carried to the grave, a large military aircraft flew over with a thunderous roar; it seemed like a final tribute to their little pilot.

For all eternity Ryan's boast will be that he never once offended God through personal sin. While Ryan's parents still miss him terribly, they are very proud to have a son who is a saint.

NOVEMBER 1 is also the feast of Saint Tracy Schmitz. Little Tracy was only about four years old when Jesus came to welcome her into his Father's house, but Tracy knew much suffering during her short lifetime.

I first came to know Tracy as "the little girl who has cancer." She was in and out of the hospital many times, but whenever she was well enough her mother or dad would carry her with them to Mass. It was obvious that Tracy was ill; chemotherapy had caused her to lose her hair, and her weary face tore many hearts to pieces, but I never remember seeing little Tracy cry.

She was a bright little girl for her age and knew that Jesus was present in the little white host in Communion. Thus, during the final months of her illness, we priests permitted little Tracy to receive Jesus in the Eucharist. How touching it was for everyone to see us break off a particle of the Sacred Host and place it on little Tracy's tongue as her father or mother held her lovingly in their arms. Jesus, I'm sure, must have been filled with joy as he came into Tracy's innocent heart.

Many tears were shed at Tracy's funeral. But deep down inside everyone knew that another saint had entered Jesus' eternal kingdom.

I LIKE TO THINK that the feast of All Saints is also "Big Mark's" feast day. A sophomore in high school, Mark stood six-foot, four-inches tall and was solid as a rock; he was a football coach's dream. Fortunately for the rest of us, he had a very gentle disposition.

I first met Mark when he and his sisters came to religious education classes. I remember well one difficult day in the classroom when no one was paying attention. Finally, I blew my stack. In a very threatening voice, I declared that everyone had better shape up. I took a deep breath and stood as tall as my 6-foot, 1-inch frame would allow, reminding the class that I was big enough to boot out anyone who didn't behave. Suddenly, out of the corner of my eye, I saw Mark sitting in the back of the room and realized the humor of the moment. "Mark," I said, "I wasn't talking to you. You can do whatever you want in here, okay? I'll leave you alone if you leave me alone."

He just smiled, and the tension in the classroom dissipated. I never did have to worry about Mark; he was always attentive and never caused a disturbance. Every Sunday I would see him with his family seated near the front of the church; they always received communion together.

One Sunday afternoon as Mark was walking along the river with some friends, the bank caved in. Suddenly, Mark saw his sister being swept under by the swift current. Without a second thought he jumped in after her and somehow managed to help her to safety. But Mark himself didn't make it.

I think of the words of Jesus when he said, "Greater love than this no man has, than that he lay down his life for his friends." I like to think that these words apply to Mark, and I like to think that he is a saint in heaven.

ON NOVEMBER 1, I think of Lucille, a middle-aged housewife and mother of a large family. In spite of her many responsibilities, Lucille was one of those women you could always count on when you needed help. Be it a parish or civic function, or just a neighbor in need, Lucille was at the door ready to pitch in almost before you realized you needed help. Yet she never remained to receive thanks or public recognition.

In spite of her busy schedule, Lucille found time each week to spend an hour with our Lord in the Blessed Sacrament. It was after her final hour of adoration that I last spoke with Lucille. I met her on the sidewalk as she was leaving church.

"Oh, Father," she said. "I'd like to ask a special favor of you. I'm going into the hospital tomorrow for minor surgery. I'll just be gone a couple of days. Would you please keep me in your prayers that everything goes well?" Then she went on to say, "I've been intending to have you out for dinner some evening. When I get home from the hospital I'll give you a call, maybe we can set up a date."

I assured Lucille that I would keep her in my prayers. But God's ways are not always our ways. Complications developed during the "minor" surgery and Lucille died suddenly on the operating table. Her husband, family, and the entire community were stunned and grief-stricken. Only the words of Jesus could offer some comfort: "Do not let your hearts be troubled. Have faith in God and faith in me. In my Father's house there are many dwelling places. Otherwise, how could I have told you I am going to prepare a place for you? I am indeed going to prepare a place for you and then I shall come back to take you with me so that where I am, you may also be."

Lucille always put her trust in the Lord; she truly tried to imitate his example of love and concern for others. I like to think that she is a saint in heaven, and that November 1 is her feast day.

† Father Joseph A. Miksch
Archdiocese of Omaha

Final Thoughts

For ANYONE CONSIDERING the priesthood, I pray that this book, and the thoughts in this chapter, become a source of inspiration as you discern your calling. These reflections are affirmations of how privileged these men feel they are to be called Catholic priests.

A PRIEST IS A NORMAL HUMAN BEING with all the weaknesses, all the temptations, and all the failures of any other man. I would tell any young man considering the priesthood to "Go for it!"

It's a great life!

It's a beautiful life!

I love it, I love every day of it. I love getting up every morning.

Nothing could be finer in my life.

† Father Robert J. Boyle
Diocese of Pittsburgh

"THE CHURCH NEEDS some humor and we priests need more humor!"

† Father Dominic J. Valla
Archdiocese of Hartford

BEING A PRIEST is more than what you do, it is what you are.

† Father Michael W. Decewicz
Diocese of Pittsburgh

IF THERE'S ONE THING I know I've learned, it's that you cannot say "no" to God! Being out among the people is the very best thing about being a priest.

† Father Frances B. Pellegrino
Diocese of Salt Lake City

THE LIFE OF A PRIEST is one of sacrifice, but it is very, very rewarding. If a priest really lives up to the ideals of the priesthood, as difficult as that is, with slips and falls and with failings, it's a great gift to the parishioners.

† Monsignor Joseph J. Granato
Archdiocese of Newark

THE BEST PART about being a priest is when I know people, and I can really touch their lives.

† Father C. Louis Martin
Archdiocese of Baltimore

THE GREATEST SATISFACTION about being a priest is that you can be there at significant and important moments in people's lives. You can help people make transitions.

† Father David Cooney, S.D.S.
Diocese of Phoenix

THE PRIESTHOOD IS EVERYTHING that I expected, and everything that I feared, but the benefits are far greater than I ever anticipated.

† Father Joseph A. Rulli
Diocese of Fort Wayne/South Bend

HOW PRIVILEGED is the priest to witness real life.

† Father C. Peter Dumont
Diocese of Manchester

The Parish Priest

N⊙ MATTER WHERE he is located, the parish priest
has to be the sharer of secrets, the carrier of burdens, the
fountain of consolation, and the pillar of strength.

Solitary, he is called father by thousands;
poor, he enriches the lives of thousands;
weak, he gives strength to thousands;
unimportant, he does things each day
whose importance cannot be told
in any tongue on earth.

He is never too busy to hear another's sorrows;
often too busy to realize his own burdens.
He is a twenty-four-hour-a-day man.

He is called from his dinner; wakened from his sleep;
disturbed at his prayers. He is at the beck and call
of any of his people.
He is the target of God's enemies,
the magnet of God's needy.

Occasionally, he attracts attention;
but usually he works unnoticed and unacclaimed
while he does the noblest work on earth—
Keeps Christ in the lives of his people.

Byzantine Catholic Serra Club of Pittsburgh

Contributors

I AM VERY GRATEFUL to all the priests who took time from their busy schedule to answer my letter and endure my interviews. A special thanks to my pastor, Father Michael Decewicz, who supported me throughout this project. And to Father Joe Miksch and Father Larry Hess, thank you for sharing so deeply your reflective insights into your ministry.

Every effort has been made to acknowledge everyone who replied to my request. Because of the overwhelming response I received, it was impossible to use all the submissions. If I have inadvertently excluded your name, I ask for your forgiveness.

Many of the priests who returned stories asked for anonymity. To them, and to all the priests listed below in alphabetical order, I thank you.

Father Louis L. Anderson
Diocese of Grand Rapids, MI

Father Richard R. Andrus, S.V.D.
Archdiocese of St. Louis, MO

Father Charles R. Antekeier
Diocese of Grand Rapids, MI

Father Richard R. Archer, O.P.
Diocese of Baton Rouge, LA

Father Kenneth Arnzen
Diocese of Boise, ID

Monsignor Stephen T. Barnett
Diocese of Sioux Falls, SD

Father Joseph J. Baxter, M.S.
Diocese of Hartford, CT

Father Gerald E. Beirne
Diocese of Providence, RI

Father Joel S. Bladt, S.T.
Diocese of Savannah, GA

Father Hugo L. Blotsky, O.S.B.
Diocese of Bismarck, ND

Father Robert J. Boyle
Diocese of Pittsburgh, PA

Father James B. Braaten
Diocese of Bismarck, ND

Father Edward E. Callanan, S.J.
Diocese of Phoenix, AZ

Father Thomas B. Campion
Archdiocese of Hartford, CT

Father Michael A. Caridi
Diocese of Pittsburgh, PA

Father William J. Carrigg
Diocese of Portland, ME

Father Roger P. Chabot
Diocese of Portland, ME

Monsignor Gerardo J. Colacicco
Archdiocese of New York, NY

Father David Cooney, S.D.S.
Diocese of Phoenix, AZ

Monsignor Francis A. Cowgill
Archdiocese of Anchorage, AK

Father Alberto R. Cutie
Archdiocese of Miami, FL

Father Joseph A. Daley
Diocese of Cheyenne, WY

Father William J. Damroth III
Archdiocese of New York, NY

Father Charles P. Davignon
Diocese of Burlington, VT

Father Michael W. Decewicz
Diocese of Pittsburgh, PA

Father David T. DeJulio
Diocese of St. Petersburg, FL

Father Leo C. Desso
Archdiocese of Anchorage, AK

Father Philip E. DeVolder
Diocese of Fort Wayne/South Bend, IN

Father Henry E. Dickson, S.S.J.
Archdiocese of Mobile, AL

Father Francis A. Diffley, M.M.
Diocese of Honolulu, HI

Father Patrick J. Dolan, Ph.D.
Archdiocese of Louisville, KY

Father C. Peter Dumont
Diocese of Manchester, NH

Monsignor John J. Enzler
Archdiocese of Washington, D.C.

Father Robert L. Erickson
Diocese of Spokane, WA

Father Samuel Esposito
Diocese of Pittsburgh, PA

Father Herbert Essig
Diocese of Joliet, IL

Father Thomas J. Extejt
Diocese of Toledo, OH

Father A. J. Fisher
Archdiocese of Anchorage, AK

Father James J. Foster
Archdiocese of St. Louis, MO

Father John A. Franey
Archdiocese of Philadelphia, PA

Father Jim D. Friedrich
Diocese of Sioux Falls, SD

Father Charles L. Fuld
Diocese of San Diego, CA

Father John A. Geinzer
Diocese of Pittsburgh, PA

Father Valmont R. Gilbert
Diocese of Portland, ME

Father Carl Gimpl
Archdiocese of Portland, OR

Father Edmund Goldbach, O.M.F.
Diocese of Grand Rapids, MI

Father Peter G. Gori, O.S.A.
Archdiocese of Boston, MA

Monsignor Joseph J. Granato
Archdiocese of Newark, NJ

Father Thomas P. Haffey
Diocese of Helena, MT

Father Larry J. Hess
Diocese of Allentown, PA

Father Raymond Hofmann, C.R.
Archdiocese of Louisville, KY

Father Carl J. Hood
Diocese of Memphis, TN

Father Paul Hruby
Archdiocese of Los Angeles, CA

Father Edward S. Jaksina
Archdiocese of Hartford, CT

Father Richard J. Janson, C.M.
Archdiocese of St. Louis, MO

Father Carl D. Johnson
Archdiocese of New York, NY

Father John T. Judie
Archdiocese of Louisville, KY

Father Mario F. Julian, O.M.F.
Archdiocese of Hartford, CT

Mr. Donald Kane
Grand Rapids, MI

Father Patrick J. Keeley, C.M.
Archdiocese of St. Louis, MO

Father Thomas L. Keenan
Diocese of Providence, RI

Father Thomas W. Keller
Diocese of Little Rock, AR

Father James F. Kinnane
Archdiocese of Hartford, CT

Father Marvin J. Klemmer
Diocese of Bismarck, ND

Father David B. Knight
Diocese of Memphis, TN

Father August Koeune
Diocese of Cheyenne, WY

Father Michael Kolodziej, O.M.F.
Diocese of Springfield, MA

Father Berchmans Konnully
Diocese of Bismarck, ND

Father John A. Koonz
Diocese of Springfield, MA

Father Ernest L. L'Heureux
Diocese of Portland, ME

Father Fred LeClaire, C.M.F.
Diocese of Phoenix, AZ

Father Charles E. Maher
Diocese of Providence, RI

Father Michael Q. Mahone
Diocese of Reno, NE

Father John A. Marcucci
Diocese of Pittsburgh, PA

Father C. Louis Martin
Archdiocese of Baltimore, MD

Father Michael T. Martine
Archdiocese of New York, NY

Father Charles O. Mason
Diocese of Grand Rapids, MI

Father Charles Massoth
Archdiocese of Oklahoma City, OK

Monsignor Robert T. McManus
Archdiocese of Philadelphia, PA

Monsignor Thomas McSweeney
Archdiocese of New York, NY

Father Francis X. Meehan
Archdiocese of Philadelphia, PA

Father August A. Melito
Diocese of Dallas, TX

Father Joseph A. Miksch
Archdiocese of Omaha, NE

Father Paul Milanowski
Diocese of Grand Rapids, MI

Monsignor James R. Moore
Archdiocese of New York, NY

Monsignor Frank G. Morfeld
Archdiocese of Denver, CO

Father Raymond Moss
Diocese of Cheyenne, WY

Father Raymond Oosdyke, O.M.F.
Diocese of Grand Rapids, MI

Father William Osborn
Diocese of Sioux Falls, SD

Father Joseph Parel
Archdiocese of Hartford, CT

Father Royal J. Parent
Diocese of Portland, ME

Father Francis B. Pellegrino
Diocese of Salt Lake City, UT

Very Rev. Joseph A. Pellegrino, V.F.
Diocese of St. Petersburg, FL

Father Thomas J. Peterman, V.F.
Diocese of Wilmington, DE

Monsignor James E. Pieper
Archdiocese of St. Louis, MO

Father John G. Proctor Jr.
Diocese of San Diego, CA

Father Alfred H. Puccinelli, S.M.
Urandi, Brazil

Father Joseph Raptosh
*Metropolitan Archeparchy of
Pittsburgh, Byzantine*

Father John F. Reardon
Archdiocese of New York, NY

Father Richard J. Reiser
Archdiocese of Omaha, NE

Father George S. Reynolds, O.P.
Diocese of Pueblo, CO

Father William V. Reynolds
Archdiocese of New York, NY

Father Hilton L. Rivet, S.J.
Diocese of Baton Rouge, LA

Father Raymond Ross, C.M.
Archdiocese of St. Louis, MO

Father Joseph A. Rulli
*Diocese of Fort Wayne/
South Bend, IN*

Father Samuel S. Sacus
Diocese of Wheeling/Charleston, WV

Father Edward R. Schleicher
Diocese of Pittsburgh, PA

Father Joseph F. Schmidt
Diocese of Boise, ID

Father Warren Schoeppe, S.J.
Diocese of Salt Lake City, UT

Father Dennis A. Schroeder
Diocese of Toledo, OH

Father Victor Seidel, S.T.S.
Diocese of Savannah, GA

Father John O'Malley Sharpe, C.M.
Diocese of Phoenix, AZ

Father Vincent J. Sheehy
Diocese of Venice, FL

Father Gary L. Sigler
*Diocese of Fort Wayne/
South Bend, IN*

Father Robert J. Sipe
Archdiocese of St. Paul, MN

Father William J. Skoneki
Archdiocese of Mobile, AL

Father Leonard A. Smith
*Diocese of Wheeling/
Charleston, WV*

Father James E. Somma
Diocese of Pittsburgh, PA

Father Antonio A. Sotelo
Diocese of Phoenix, AZ

Father Charles W. Speicher, Ph.D.
Diocese of Pittsburgh, PA

Father Dennis Stehly
Archdiocese of St. Louis, MO

Father Ralph H. Talkin, S.J.
Diocese of Cheyenne, WY

Father Richard D. Tero
Archdiocese of Anchorage, AK

Father Michael J. Tracey
Diocese of Biloxi, MS

Father Michael Tyson, O.M.F.
Archdiocese of Washington, D.C.

Father Benedetto P. Vaghetto
Diocese of Pittsburgh, PA

Father Anthony C. Vainavicz
Diocese of Grand Rapids, MI

Father Dominic J. Valla
Archdiocese of Hartford, CT

Father Louis F. Vallone
Diocese of Pittsburgh, PA

Father James L. Vance
Archdiocese of Santa Fe, NM

Father Leo V. Vanyo
Diocese of Pittsburgh, PA

Father Henry C. Vavasseur
Diocese of Baton Rouge, LA

Father Thomas S. Vesbit
Diocese of Grand Rapids, MI

Father John C. Vojtek
Diocese of Pittsburgh, PA

Father Philip J. Waters, O.S.B.
Archdiocese of Newark, NJ

Father James R. Wilson
Diocese of Boise, ID

Father Robert J. Zajdel
Diocese of Pittsburgh, PA